CONTENTS

Published by CGP

Editors:
Claire Boulter
Holly Corfield-Carr
Heather Gregson
Anthony Muller
Holly Poynton

Contributors:
Jane Harrison
Kevin Smith

With thanks to Luke von Kotze and Elisabeth Sanderson for the proofreading,
and Laura Jakubowski and Laura Stoney for the copyright research.

Russian translations by Vicky Hoof and Joe Burrows.

Acknowledgements:

Cover Illustration by Aimee Seaver - http://aimeeseaver.daportfolio.com/

With thanks to Rex Features for permission to use the image on page 1.

With thanks to Mary Evans Picture Library for permission to use the images on pages 2, 6, 9 and 44.

With thanks to iStockphoto.com for permission to use the images on pages 3, 7, 15, 17, 18, 20, 24, 25, 26, 27, 28, 30, 31, 32, 34, 37, 47 and 48.

With thanks to The Kobal Collection for permission to use the images on pages 3, 14, 19, 22, 38, 43 and 46.

With thanks to Getty Images for permission to use the image on page 39.

Animalism flag on page 50 © A12 (Aldo)

Page 1: The Staff of the October Revolution, 1934 (oil on canvas) by Svarog, Vasily Semyonovich (1883-1946)
State Museum and Exhibition Centre ROSIZO, Moscow/ The Bridgeman Art Library

Page 5: Pigs Type, scene from the 1954 animated film of 'Animal Farm' adapted from the book by George Orwell (1903-50)
by Halas & Batchelor (20th century) © Halas & Batchelor Collection Ltd./ The Bridgeman Art Library

Page 8: Leon Trotsky (b/w photo) by Russian Photographer, (20th century)
Private Collection/ Peter Newark Historical Pictures/ The Bridgeman Art Library

Page 31: To Our Dear Stalin, the Nation, 1949 (litho) by Russian School, (20th century)
Musee de l'Armee, Brussels, Belgium/ Patrick Lorette/ The Bridgeman Art Library

Page 42: 1st May, Stalin (1879-1953) Holds a Child in his Arms, 1952 (colour litho)
by Resetnikov, Fedor Pavlovic (1906-1983) Private Collection/ Archives Charmet/ The Bridgeman Art Library

Every effort has been made to locate copyright holders and obtain permission to reproduce sources.
For those sources where it has been difficult to trace the copyright holder of the work, we would be grateful
for information. If any copyright holder would like us to make an amendment to the acknowledgements,
please notify us and we will gladly update the book at the next reprint. Thank you.

ISBN: 978 1 84762 667 7
Website: www.cgpbooks.co.uk
Printed by Elanders Ltd, Newcastle upon Tyne.
Clipart from CorelDRAW®

Based on the classic CGP style created by Richard Parsons.

Introduction to 'Animal Farm' and George Orwell

'Animal Farm' is about a **Revolution** that went **Wrong**

- *Animal Farm* is a novel about an <u>animal uprising</u> on a farm in England.

- Although it's fictional, it's based on <u>real events</u> — it's an <u>allegory</u> of the Russian Revolution.

The real events of the Russian Revolution

1) In October 1917, <u>Vladimir Lenin</u> led a <u>revolution</u> against the Russian government. He wanted the <u>working classes</u> to have more <u>power</u>.

2) After Lenin died, <u>Stalin</u> took <u>power</u> and became a <u>dictator</u>. Lenin's vision was completely <u>destroyed</u>.

A picture showing the planning of the October Revolution, 1917

George Orwell believed in **Equality**

- George Orwell wrote *Animal Farm* in response to Stalin's <u>corruption</u> of <u>communism</u>. The Russian Revolution had failed and life in Russia <u>wasn't equal</u>.

- He wanted to show that a <u>revolutionary leader</u> could be <u>corrupted</u> by <u>power</u> and that this could happen in any country, <u>not just in Russia</u>.

1903	Born in India as <u>Eric Arthur Blair</u>.
1907	Moved to England.
1922	Joined the Indian Police in Burma.
1927	Returned to England.
1933	Published his <u>first book</u>, 'Down and Out in Paris and London' under the name <u>George Orwell</u>.
1945	Published '<u>Animal Farm</u>'. Several publishers refused to print it because it was so <u>controversial</u>. After publication it became a <u>huge success</u>.
1949	Wrote '1984' — another <u>political novel</u>.
1950	Died, aged 46 from <u>tuberculosis</u>.

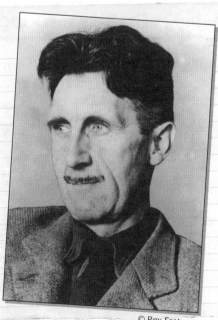

Background Information

'Animal Farm' is set **Somewhere** in **England**

Here are the <u>key locations</u> in the novel:

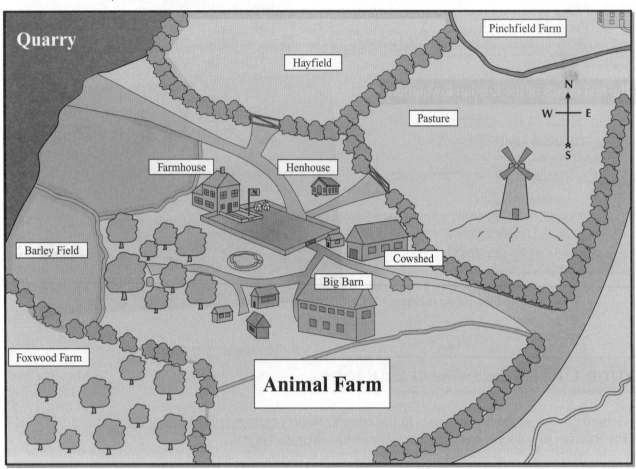

Quarry
Pinchfield Farm
Hayfield
Pasture
Farmhouse
Henhouse
Barley Field
Cowshed
Big Barn
Foxwood Farm
Animal Farm

N
W — E
S

Life under **Stalin** was **Tough**

- Stalin was a <u>dictator</u> — he ruled Russia <u>alone</u> and had <u>absolute power</u> over the Russian people.

Forced Labourers in Russia

- He used <u>fear</u> to stay in <u>control</u> — people were arrested, imprisoned or executed <u>without warning</u>.

- He used <u>propaganda</u> to develop a '<u>cult of personality</u>' — this meant that he created an idealised <u>public image</u> to increase his <u>popularity</u>.

- The Russian people <u>worked harder</u> and <u>suffered more</u> under Stalin, but <u>benefited less</u>.

Who's Who in 'Animal Farm'

Napoleon...

...is a fierce boar who always gets his own way. He leads the revolution, but the power goes to his head.

© iStockphoto.com/Christopher Mansfield

Squealer...

...is Napoleon's right-hand man and is in charge of propaganda. He's a very persuasive speaker.

© HALLMARK/TNT/ANIMAL FARM PRODUCTION
COURTESY THE KOBAL COLLECTION

Snowball...

...is clever, brave and enthusiastic. Napoleon thinks Snowball is a threat and chases him off the farm.

© HALLMARK/TNT/ANIMAL FARM PRODUCTION
COURTESY THE KOBAL COLLECTION

Old Major...

...is the principled old boar who starts the revolution.

© iStockphoto.com/Nancy Nehring

Boxer...

...is a hard worker but a slow thinker. He tries to solve problems by working harder, and never doubts Napoleon.

© iStockphoto.com/Russell Du parcq

Benjamin...

...is a cynical donkey who does no more than he has to on the farm.

© iStockphoto.com/Ivonne Wierink-vanWetten

Mollie...

...is a vain, pretty horse who cares more about herself than the revolution.

© HALLMARK/TNT/ANIMAL FARM PRODUCTION
COURTESY THE KOBAL COLLECTION

Moses...

...is a religious raven who tells the animals tales of 'Sugarcandy Mountain'. The pigs call him a liar but let him stay on the farm.

© iStockphoto.com/step2626

Clover...

...is a kind, motherly horse. She worries about the other animals on the farm.

© iStockphoto.com/Sylwia Kachel

Mr Jones...

...is a cruel, drunken farmer. His animals rebel against him, chasing him off his farm.

'Animal Farm' — Plot Summary

© Aimee Seaver

'Animal Farm'... what happens when?

Here's a little recap of the <u>main events</u> of 'Animal Farm'. It's a good idea to learn <u>what happens when</u>, so that in the exam you can easily flick to the passage or quote you want to write about.

Chapters One to Three — *The Revolution*

- <u>Old Major</u> calls the animals to a meeting. He tells them about his <u>dream</u> of the animals living in <u>harmony</u> and working <u>only for themselves</u>.

- Major <u>dies</u>, but when Jones forgets to feed the animals, the pigs lead a <u>rebellion</u> against him and <u>chase him away</u>.

- After the revolution, Snowball and Napoleon <u>take charge</u> and turn Major's vision into <u>Animalism</u>. They draw up <u>seven commandments</u> to guide the animals.

- The next harvest is <u>incredibly successful</u>. It's <u>hard going</u> but all the animals <u>work together</u>.

- The pigs <u>steal</u> the cows' <u>milk</u> and the <u>apples</u> to keep for <u>themselves</u>. They explain that they need the food because they're the <u>brains</u> on the farm.

Chapters Four to Five — *Conflict on the Farm*

- <u>News</u> of the animals' successful revolution <u>spreads</u> to neighbouring farms owned by Frederick and Pilkington. They <u>help Jones</u> try to recapture his farm.

- The humans attack and Snowball <u>bravely leads</u> the animals to a victory at the <u>Battle of the Cowshed</u>.

- Snowball and Napoleon <u>disagree over everything</u> and tensions run high. Snowball wants to <u>build a windmill</u>, but Napoleon urinates over the plans.

- At the final windmill debate, Napoleon <u>sets his dogs</u> on Snowball and he's <u>chased</u> from the farm.

- Napoleon announces that he's going to <u>build the windmill</u> after all.

Chapters Six to Eight — *Napoleon's New Regime*

- The animals <u>work harder</u> and <u>eat less</u> under Napoleon.

- Napoleon starts <u>ignoring</u> the principles of Animalism, <u>trading with humans</u> and sleeping in the <u>farmhouse beds</u>.

- Squealer <u>changes the commandments</u> to suit the pigs' needs.

- When the completed windmill falls down in a storm, <u>Napoleon blames Snowball</u>.

- The farm has a bad harvest. Napoleon tells the hens that he's going to <u>sell their eggs</u> to raise some money — when they <u>refuse</u>, he <u>starves them</u> until they give in. To prevent further rebellion, Napoleon forces many animals to confess that they're working with Snowball, then <u>executes</u> them.

- Napoleon <u>sells timber</u> to Frederick, who pays him with <u>forged notes</u>. Frederick then <u>invades the farm</u> and <u>blows up the windmill</u>. After a great struggle, the animals win the <u>Battle of the Windmill</u>.

Chapters Nine to Ten — *Back to Square One*

- The animals continue to <u>work hard</u>, and rebuild the windmill. They're <u>starving</u>, while the pigs get <u>fatter</u> and <u>lazier</u>.

- Napoleon introduces <u>new rules</u> that <u>benefit the pigs</u>, but not the other animals.

- <u>Boxer</u>, the farm's <u>most loyal worker</u>, collapses from <u>overwork</u> and is <u>sold</u> to the knacker's yard.

- Napoleon becomes more like Jones — he walks on <u>two legs</u>, <u>wears clothes</u> and <u>carries a whip</u>.

- All the commandments are <u>removed</u> and replaced with just one — "<u>ALL ANIMALS ARE EQUAL, BUT SOME ARE MORE EQUAL THAN OTHERS</u>."

- Napoleon <u>invites the humans</u> to the farm to <u>play cards</u>. At the end, the animals can't tell the <u>pigs</u> and <u>humans apart</u>.

Animal Farm — *funny farm more like...*

Animal Farm may be a smallish novel but there's so much juicy stuff in it. It's got something for everyone — dramatic battles, thieving and corruption, evil talking super-pigs, as well as a hidden political message. If you're still not 100% clear on the plot, turn to the back of the book for the cartoon. Read on, comrades!

Context: Russia before the Revolution

This section gives you a bit of <u>context</u> to *Animal Farm*. Orwell isn't <u>just</u> writing about an evil talking pig who starts wearing clothes, drinking whisky and playing cards. His message is much <u>deeper</u> than that...

*Animal Farm is an **Allegory***

1) *Animal Farm* is an <u>allegory</u>, which means that the main characters and events of the story <u>represent real people</u> and <u>events</u> in Soviet Russia. Orwell <u>simplifies</u> events in *Animal Farm* to make his message <u>clearer</u>.

2) The story is based on <u>Russian history</u>, from around <u>1917 to 1943</u>, four years before the <u>Cold War</u>.

Farmer Jones** represents the **Unpopular Tsar

1) Tsar Nicholas II had ruled Russia since 1894.
He was <u>powerful</u>, <u>unpopular</u> and had <u>absolute authority</u>.

2) Most of the country's wealth and land was owned by a <u>small noble class</u>. Most of the rest of the population were <u>peasants</u>.

> **Farmer Jones**
> - Farmer Jones has <u>absolute control</u> over the animals.
>   This represents the Tsar's <u>power</u> over the Russian people.
> - Jones lives in <u>luxury</u> while the animals work hard for his <u>benefit</u>.

ТОВ. Ленин ОЧИЩАЕТ землю от нечисти.

Lenin sweeping away the unpopular Tsar and the ruling classes.

***Old Major** represents Lenin's **Revolutionary Ideas**...*

1) A <u>radical</u> party called the Bolsheviks wanted to <u>end</u> this <u>inequality</u>.

2) This group was led by Lenin (see p. 7). He wanted a <u>revolution</u> to <u>overthrow</u> the Tsar and called for an <u>end</u> to capitalism (see below). He wanted to take <u>power</u> on behalf of <u>the workers</u>.

> **Old Major**
> Old Major also tells the animals to <u>rise up</u> against their <u>human</u> masters.

*...and Marx's view on **Capitalism***

1) Capitalism is an economic system based on <u>business</u> — it's selling things to make a <u>profit</u>.

2) <u>Marx</u>, a political thinker, said this was <u>wrong</u> because those who did the work were poor while the business owners were getting rich. He said that a <u>workers' revolution</u> would end inequality. After the revolution, <u>production</u> would benefit everyone and everything would be <u>shared</u> — this is called <u>communism</u>.

> **Old Major**
> - Old Major also warns of the <u>dangers</u> of <u>trading</u> with humans.
> - He's proven <u>right</u> in the end — when Napoleon decides to <u>trade</u> with Frederick, Frederick pays him in <u>forged</u> bank notes.

Make sure you learn the historical background — it's easy Marx...

I know you're probably thinking "but I didn't sign up for history..." — unfortunately, you need to know the context to understand the plot of *Animal Farm* and what Orwell is saying. You just gotta grin and bear it for six more pages.

Context: Lenin and the Revolution

Lots of the characters in *Animal Farm* link to Russia in some way. In the novel, Major is a <u>mixture</u> of Marx <u>and</u> Lenin. Two parts, that's just greedy — but then, what else can you expect from a pig...

*Like the **Russian People**, the animals **Rebel***

1) The Tsar <u>gave up the throne</u> in February 1917 because the Russian people were <u>rioting</u>. A <u>provisional government</u> was set up to replace him.

The Rebellion
- Just like the Russian people, the animals <u>rebel</u> against their ruler.
- Jones is taken <u>by surprise</u> and the animals <u>quickly</u> defeat him.

2) Lenin thought the <u>Bolsheviks</u> were the best people to <u>lead</u> Russia. Later that year, they seized <u>power</u> and overthrew the ruling classes without much <u>opposition</u>.

3) An <u>election</u> was held for a new parliament, but when the Bolsheviks <u>failed to win</u> a majority vote they <u>closed down</u> the Assembly.

4) The Bolsheviks became the <u>Communist Party</u>, the only legal party in Russia.

Orwell simplifies events in Russia to make his message about revolutionary leaders clearer — remember it's an allegory, not a history book.

The Pigs
- The Bolsheviks quickly became the <u>only</u> political party. Soon after the rebellion, the pigs also <u>take charge</u> of running the farm.
- At first, the animals <u>seem</u> to be <u>equal</u> — but as time goes by, Napoleon gets rid of any <u>opposition</u>. It's the end of <u>democracy</u>.

*Old Major shares lots of **Lenin's Key Strengths***

1) Lenin's <u>organisation</u> and <u>leadership</u> transformed the Bolshevik party. He had a <u>sensible</u> and <u>realistic approach</u> to problems.

2) When Lenin died in 1924, Stalin put Lenin's body on <u>public display</u> to associate himself with Lenin's ideas.

3) Lenin had a <u>right-hand man</u> called <u>Trotsky</u>, who seemed the obvious choice to be Lenin's successor, but Stalin <u>pushed him out</u>.

Old Major
- Old Major shares lots of Lenin's <u>qualities</u> — he <u>encourages</u> the animals to <u>rebel</u> and his memory <u>comforts</u> the animals.
- Like Stalin, Napoleon puts <u>Major's skull</u> on public display.
- <u>Snowball</u> represents <u>Trotsky</u> in *Animal Farm* — after Major's death, Snowball seems to be the <u>likely</u> leader of the farm.

A statue of Lenin

For extra points — What were the Tsar's children called? Tsardines...

If you thought that was a bit fishy, you'd be correct. I made it up. Good joke though. The key to the Bolsheviks' success was the speed of the revolution. Before anyone knew what had happened, Lenin was already in charge. Clever.

Context: Trotsky

Trotsky held many <u>important roles</u> in the Communist Party, but his most famous role was as <u>leader of the army</u>. <u>Snowball</u> represents Trotsky, and it's quite funny really, because he's got trotters. Hahahahaha... oh dear.

*Trotsky was a **Brilliant Leader** and so is **Snowball**...*

1) After the revolution, there was a <u>civil war</u> between the <u>Bolsheviks</u> and people still <u>loyal to the Tsar</u>.

2) Trotsky proved that he was a <u>good</u> leader by organising a <u>powerful</u> army. Under <u>Trotsky's leadership</u>, the Bolsheviks <u>won</u> the civil war.

> **Battle of the Cowshed**
>
> - This should ring some (cow) bells — it's the <u>Battle of the Cowshed</u>.
> - When Jones returns to <u>seize</u> the farm, Snowball's strategies mean that the animals are <u>prepared</u>. Snowball is an <u>organised</u>, <u>resourceful</u> military leader.

*...but they both have a **Ruthless Streak***

1) When a <u>mutiny</u> broke out on a Russian naval base, Trotsky sent in the <u>army</u>.

2) The army <u>attacked</u>, and <u>captured</u> the base in a brutal battle. Many rebels were <u>killed</u>.

A mutiny is a rebellion or uprising against people in authority, usually on a ship.

> **Snowball**
>
> - Snowball's <u>commitment</u> to Animalism means that he can be <u>coldhearted</u>.
> - He tells Boxer that "War is war. The only good human being is a dead one."

*There was a **Power Struggle** in **Russia***

1) <u>Trotsky</u> was capable and <u>popular</u> with the <u>army</u> and <u>Party members</u>. His <u>main rival</u> was Joseph <u>Stalin</u>, who had built a power base 'behind the scenes' in his work as <u>General Secretary</u> of the Party.

2) <u>Lenin</u> said <u>Trotsky</u> was <u>arrogant</u> but <u>good</u> at his job, and that <u>Stalin</u> should be <u>removed from office</u> because he was <u>too rude</u> and <u>ambitious</u>.

Trotsky at his desk

> **Napoleon and Snowball**
>
> The <u>power struggle</u> between Stalin and Trotsky is mirrored in the <u>leadership battle</u> between Napoleon and Snowball after Major dies. Snowball's <u>popular</u> campaign is no match for Napoleon's <u>violent tactics</u>.

3) After Lenin's death, Stalin went on to <u>seize power</u> from right under Trotsky's nose, simply through <u>clever organisation</u> and <u>planning</u>. Trotsky didn't even realise Stalin was a threat until it was <u>too late</u>.

You've got to fight! For your right! To _{run the Communist} *Paaaaarrrrrtttttyyyyyy!*

Yes, those quiet bookwormy fellows are always the most dangerous... For all Trotsky's merits, his arrogance was ultimately his downfall. He underestimated Stalin's power base — a pretty serious mistake to make. Silly boy.

Context: Stalin

Stalin was the <u>outsider</u> in the leadership battle — Lenin didn't even like him. Yet he managed to <u>seize control</u>. This page will tell you how. If you hadn't guessed yet, <u>Napoleon = Stalin</u>. Yup, they're both big meanies...

Napoleon represents *Stalin* in the *Allegory*

1) Stalin was an <u>organiser</u>. He was <u>General Secretary</u> of the Communist Party — he could <u>control</u> who was given government roles, and chose people <u>loyal</u> to him.

2) His <u>rivals</u> didn't have the same <u>support</u> and by the late 1920s, they <u>were all voted out</u> of power.

Napoleon
- It might not seem like Napoleon <u>does much</u> at first — but he's secretly <u>training</u> the puppies.
- He <u>surrounds himself</u> with <u>loyal followers</u> in a similar way to Stalin, leaving Snowball <u>isolated</u>.

Stalin used his *Position* to *Remove Trotsky*

1) Trotsky was <u>thrown out</u> of the Party and forced to <u>leave</u> Russia in 1929.

Napoleon <u>expels</u> Snowball from the farm.

2) Trotsky became a '<u>non-person</u>' — his name was <u>removed</u> from history books and his picture was rubbed out of photos.

Napoleon <u>blames</u> any problems on Snowball and <u>spreads rumours</u> that Snowball's been working for Jones.

Lenin and Stalin sitting together on a bench. Stalin was keen to spread such images.

3) Stalin created a '<u>cult of personality</u>'. Photographs were <u>altered</u> to show Stalin and Lenin as friends. Stalin spread <u>propaganda</u> about his own <u>great leadership</u> and banned <u>criticism</u> against him. He <u>rewrote</u> history so that he played a more <u>important part</u> in the <u>revolution</u>.

Squealer spreads <u>propaganda</u> about Napoleon's <u>great leadership</u> and <u>rewrites history</u>.

Napoleon's Regime symbolises *Stalin's Dictatorship*

1) By 1929, Stalin was in <u>complete control</u> of the Communist Party and Russia. His policies were often completely different from <u>communist ideas</u>.

2) Even though he was <u>undisputed leader</u> of Russia, he became terrified that others wanted to overthrow him. However, most people lived in <u>fear</u> and were <u>unable</u> to speak out.

Napoleon
- Like Stalin, Napoleon becomes a <u>dictator</u>. He has <u>absolute power</u> on Animal Farm.
- He <u>undermines</u> the <u>commandments</u> one by one and changes them to suit him.
- The animals become increasingly <u>scared</u> but can't, or won't, <u>stand up</u> to him.

Propaganda and scapegoats — Stalin's key tactics...
The similarities between our piggy friend and Stalin are really mounting up — both use propaganda, both use scapegoats, both get their own way and both turned away from their ideals to get what they want. Not such a coincidence...

Context: Life Under Stalin

It's hard to say which would be worse — living under Stalin or Napoleon. They're both evil <u>dictators</u>, <u>power mad</u>, <u>paranoid</u> and <u>pompous</u>. But choosing which one I'd rather have in my sausages, that's a bit easier.

Orwell uses *Napoleon* to criticise *Stalin's Violence*

1) Stalin <u>ordered</u> a <u>purge</u> of people he believed were part of a <u>conspiracy</u> against him.

2) Many 'old' communists were accused of plotting with the exiled Trotsky, and were <u>arrested</u> and charged in '<u>show trials</u>'. They were <u>forced</u> by torture or threats to <u>confess</u> to betraying Stalin.

3) Anyone suspected of <u>disloyalty</u> to Stalin was taken away by the <u>NKVD</u> (the new secret police) and <u>shot</u> or sent to <u>labour camps</u>. As many as 10 million people <u>died</u>.

> ### Napoleon and the Executions
> - Napoleon holds similar <u>trials</u> when Snowball is said to be plotting against him <u>in exile</u>.
> - He forces animals to <u>admit</u> to working with Snowball, then <u>executes</u> them in public.
> - Even if Napoleon knows that the animals <u>aren't</u> conspiring against him, he wants to prove his <u>power</u> and <u>scare</u> anyone who might try to <u>rebel</u>.

Like the *Russian Peasants*, the *Hens* are treated *Badly*

1) Russian peasants were forced to <u>collectivise</u> — everything was to be shared with the state.

2) They <u>resisted</u>, especially the kulaks (richer peasants).

3) Stalin sent troops to <u>attack</u> them. Many <u>burned</u> their own crops and <u>killed</u> livestock in protest. This led to a <u>famine</u> in the 1930s.

> ### The Hens
> - When the hens are told to <u>sell</u> their eggs to <u>help</u> the farm, they smash the eggs in <u>protest</u>.
> - Napoleon <u>starves</u> the hens until they <u>give in</u>.

Like *Napoleon*, *Stalin* tried to create *Alliances*

1) In 1939, Stalin signed a <u>pact with Hitler</u> to form an alliance between Russia and Germany, but Hitler <u>betrayed</u> Stalin and <u>invaded</u> Russia in 1941. Russia <u>stopped the invasion</u> but many Russians <u>suffered</u>.

2) After the war, Russia <u>signed a pact</u> with Britain and the US to <u>protect their interests</u>. The US and Britain also thought that such a deal would <u>benefit their countries</u>.

An alliance is an agreement of friendship between two countries.

> ### The Pigs and the Humans
> This reflects the <u>relationship</u> between the <u>pigs</u> and the farmers. They start as <u>enemies</u> — but they become <u>friends</u>. At the end of the book they <u>fall out</u> again over cheating at a card game...

Even in Russia, some groups were "more equal" than others...

Communism was supposed to be about equality, but those high up in the Party got the best goods and services. Some workers got promoted due to improved education, but not everyone did. This inequality is echoed in *Animal Farm*.

Parallels — History and the Novel

Here's a handy summary for you to refer to when reading the novel. The things I do for you...

Marxism

1) The Communist Party believed in Marx's ideas. Marx said that the upper classes took advantage of the lower classes by paying them low wages, while the rich kept most of the money...

1917

2) Lenin, leader of the Bolsheviks, seizes power and overthrows the Provisional Government.

3) Lenin and Trotsky set up a Communist society. They want Russia to be fairer.

1918 - 1921

4) There's a civil war in Russia between the Bolsheviks and people loyal to the Tsar. The Bolsheviks, led by Trotsky, win the war.

1924 - 1927

5) Lenin's death causes a leadership battle between Trotsky and Stalin. Stalin wins and forces Trotsky out of Russia.

1932 - 1936

6) Stalin's collectivisation policy creates many famines. Peasants fight the changes, but conditions get worse.

7) Stalin uses propaganda to become a powerful dictator. People are encouraged to idolise him.

8) Stalin invents a conspiracy against him, and uses it as an excuse to torture and execute his enemies.

1941

9) With Russia under threat, Stalin negotiates with Germany for protection. Germany betrays Russia by (unsuccessfully) invading.

1943

10) Russia, Britain and the US become allies. The alliance is short — no one trusts each other, and four years later the Cold War begins.

Chapter 1

1) Major's ideas are similar to Marxism. He says that Man takes advantage of the animals who do all the work for no reward. This idea forms the basis of Animalism.

Chapter 2

2) The animals rise up against Jones and chase him from the farm.

3) The pigs try to create an equal society, in which "All animals are equal".

Chapter 4

4) Farmer Jones and his men attack Animal Farm at the Battle of the Cowshed. Snowball leads the animals to victory.

Chapter 5

5) Napoleon and Snowball fight over the way the farm should be run, then Napoleon drives Snowball from the farm.

Chapters 6 - 7

6) Napoleon tells the hens to sell their eggs for the collective good. The hens smash their eggs in protest.

7) Napoleon uses fear and propaganda to make himself a popular dictator.

8) Napoleon uses the windmill's destruction as an excuse to kill animals who he claims have been working for Snowball.

Chapter 8

9) Napoleon's business deals with Frederick backfire. The animals are paid in forged notes and Frederick attacks the farm.

Chapter 10

10) The relationship between the pigs and the farmers becomes friendly. The friendship is short-lived when each side cheats at cards.

Section One — Background and Context

Practice Questions

What is history? Well in this case his-story is *Animal Farm*. Yes, that joke was so terrible I bet you almost groaned out loud. If you're not groaning already, you will be in about 5 seconds... that's right, it's time for some joyous questions.

Quick Questions

Q1   Briefly explain why the ruling classes were unpopular.

Q2   Briefly describe the main difference between capitalism and communism.

Q3   Why did Lenin not want Stalin to take charge? Give two reasons.

Q4   What was Stalin's role in the Communist Party before he took control?

Q5   Give three examples of how Stalin used propaganda to promote himself above his rivals.

Q6   Suggest one possible reason for Stalin's purges?

Q7   How did the peasants resist collectivisation?

In-depth Questions

Q1   How was Farmer Jones' control over Manor Farm similar to Tsar Nicholas II's rule over Russia?

Q2   In what ways is Animalism similar to Marxism?

Q3   Describe two characteristics that Trotsky and Snowball share.

Q4   Describe two characteristics that Stalin and Napoleon share.

Q5   Compare the types of propaganda used by Stalin and the types of propaganda used by Squealer.

Q6   Choose one conflict from the novel and explain how it mirrors a real-life event in Russia.

Q7   Based on what you've read, do you think *Animal Farm* was 'more equal' than Stalin's Russia? Give reasons for your answer.

Analysis of Chapter One — The Dream

By now you should know what happens in *Animal Farm*. If you don't, then go directly to the <u>intro section</u>. Do not pass go, do not collect £200. This section is all about analysing the chapters for <u>deeper meaning</u>...

Old Major has a *Dream*...

1) Old Major calls a <u>meeting</u> of all the animals after Jones has gone to bed <u>drunk</u>.

2) The speech that Major gives has <u>five main purposes</u>:

- To show them that "<u>Man</u> is the only <u>real enemy</u>", because he does <u>nothing</u> but takes the benefit from the animals' <u>hard work</u>.

- To <u>warn</u> them against taking up the <u>evils</u> of <u>Man</u> e.g. alcohol.

- To <u>encourage rebellion</u> — "That is my message to you, comrades: Rebellion!" He tells the animals to <u>spread this message</u>.

- To call for "<u>perfect unity</u>" and <u>equality</u> among all animals.

- To teach them a revolutionary song — '<u>Beasts of England</u>'.

By showing how badly the animals are treated, Orwell makes the reader sympathise with them and their cause.

Allegory

Major's speech echoes <u>Marx's</u> ideas about <u>communism</u> (see p. 6).

...but there are already *Problems*

Theme — Animalism

Even at the <u>birth of Animalism</u> there are already <u>problems of equality</u>.

1) When Major gives his speech, the dogs and pigs get the <u>best position</u> (in front of the platform), which suggests that they think they're <u>superior</u>.

2) They're also the only animals <u>clever enough</u> to learn 'Beasts of England' within a few minutes. This shows that they have an <u>advantage</u> over the others, even before the rebellion.

3) After Major talks about equality and unity, it's ironic that the dogs <u>chase</u> the <u>wild rats</u> that live in the barn.

Orwell Introduces the *Characters' Personalities*

Orwell uses the meeting in the barn to describe the main characters' <u>personalities</u> and give the reader a glimpse of how the characters might <u>respond</u> to events <u>later in the novel</u>:

1) Boxer and Clover <u>take great care</u> entering the barn, in case they step on any small animals "concealed in the straw". <u>Dishonest characters</u> could <u>take advantage</u> of this kindness.

2) Boxer is also described as "<u>not of first-rate intelligence</u>" — he's got a <u>steady character</u> and a tremendous <u>desire</u> and <u>ability to work</u>. This is ultimately his <u>downfall</u>.

3) Mollie and the cat are <u>selfish</u> and <u>don't care</u> about the idea of a <u>revolution</u>.

Why the long face — I'm a slave to a cruel master. And I'm a horse...

The humans' treatment of the animals is described in great detail in Chapter One to show the reader that a revolution is a good idea. Make sure you re-read Major's speech — the old pig's ideas are really important to the rest of the novel.

Analysis of Chapter Two — The Revolution

The first two chapters <u>set the scene</u> for the rest of the novel. There's lots of <u>hints</u> about what's to come, but things haven't even begun to get bad yet... So much for a happy ending — there could at least be a happy beginning.

The *Animals Prepare* for *Rebellion*

Theme — Education

The animals that <u>take charge</u> are the ones that are <u>educated</u> (see p. 38).

1) The pigs are "generally recognised as being the <u>cleverest</u>". They take Major's ideas and turn them into <u>Animalism</u>.

2) When the rebellion comes, the animals attack "with <u>one accord</u>" and <u>chase Jones</u> from the farm. After the victory, they destroy the <u>symbols</u> of their <u>oppression</u>.

3) After the revolution, most of the animals are <u>happier</u> and the farm's more <u>successful</u>.

4) The initial <u>positive results</u> of the revolution show that <u>Orwell</u> thought that the uprising was a <u>good thing</u> — it's the way the pigs go about <u>taking control</u> which he's <u>criticising</u>.

Not all the animals *Understand Old Major's Ideas...*

1) Some animals <u>resent</u> the new rules, feeling a "<u>duty of loyalty</u>" to Jones. Mollie is <u>reluctant</u> to lose her sugar, and is found admiring herself in a mirror with one of Mrs Jones' ribbons.

2) Some animals prefer to believe in <u>Moses' stories</u> about <u>Sugarcandy Mountain</u> than in Animalism (see p. 34).

3) Most of the animals <u>don't understand</u> the ideas behind Animalism and they <u>can't read</u> the <u>commandments</u> that the pigs write on the wall.

© HALLMARK/TNT/ANIMAL FARM PRODUCTION COURTESY THE KOBAL COLLECTION

This <u>lack of understanding</u> threatens Animal Farm's future. If the animals don't understand the principles, they won't be able to <u>uphold them</u> — the <u>ruling pigs</u> will be able to <u>change Animalism</u> as they please.

...and not *Everyone* is *Equal*

Theme — Animalism

Once the rebellion's over, the pigs carry on <u>controlling</u> the animals instead of <u>encouraging equality</u>. Orwell said that revolutions <u>only worked</u> if the people knew to "<u>chuck out their leaders</u>" once they'd <u>done their job</u>.

1) The pigs <u>take charge</u> after the rebellion — so there's already <u>inequality</u>.

2) When the milk goes missing, the reader suspects that the pigs are <u>responsible</u>.

3) This shows that the pigs are already putting <u>themselves</u> before the <u>others</u>. It also shows how <u>trusting</u> the other animals are because they don't <u>confront the pigs</u>.

4) Orwell hasn't said that Animalism is going to go <u>horribly wrong</u>, but he introduces enough <u>doubt</u> in the first two chapters to make us think it's <u>not going to be easy</u>.

I never trusted pigs — even before I read Animal Farm...

Look at them, plotting away... Gives me the creeps. You can already see themes starting to emerge in this chapter, and there's some pretty big hints about what's to come — the pigs can't be trusted and the animals don't understand Animalism.

Analysis of Chapter Three — Milk and Apples

Chapter Three, or as I like to call it — The Mystery of the Missing Milk. I think the butler did it. The <u>problems of Animalism</u> become <u>clearer</u> in this chapter and by the end of the novel they snowball (ha) out of control...

Even **Early On** in the **Revolution, Not Everyone's Happy**...

1) Most of the animals <u>help</u> with the farm work — it's <u>tough going</u> but the rewards are <u>worth it</u>.

2) Not all the animals put <u>Animalism first</u> — their <u>selfishness</u> goes against the <u>principles</u> of the revolution and shows that "perfect unity" isn't <u>easy</u>:

   - Mollie <u>wakes up late</u> and <u>leaves work early</u> saying she has a "<u>stone in her hoof</u>".
   - The cat is <u>hardly ever</u> seen doing work and only turns up at <u>meal-times</u>.

3) Napoleon and Snowball <u>disagree</u> on almost <u>every issue</u>, causing <u>further problems</u>:

   - Snowball wants to <u>educate all the animals</u>, but Napoleon only wants to <u>focus on the young</u>.
   - Napoleon has "<u>no interest</u>" in Snowball's committees and is clearly developing his <u>own agenda</u>.

The **Social Classes** become more **Obvious**

1) The pigs are the <u>only ones</u> who <u>suggest resolutions</u> at the Sunday meetings.

2) They <u>separate themselves</u> from the other animals and set up their own "headquarters". They already <u>behave</u> as if they are <u>superior</u> and <u>deserve</u> to be treated better than the others.

3) It's revealed that the pigs <u>did take the milk</u> and the extra <u>apples</u>. Squealer <u>justifies</u> this using:

   - **PROPAGANDA** — he says that the pigs did it for the <u>benefit of the farm</u>. They need the apples and milk for their "well-being" which is <u>important</u> because they're "brainworkers".
   - **FEAR** — He <u>threatens</u> them with the <u>farm's failure</u> if the pigs can't work properly.

Milk and **Apples** is a **Key Turning Point**

1) This is the <u>first time</u> the pigs <u>use their authority</u> so openly.

2) It's also the first time Squealer uses <u>propaganda</u> as a way of <u>controlling</u> the animals' <u>thoughts</u>.

3) Nobody stands up and says that the pigs were <u>wrong</u>.

© iStockphoto.com/Thomas Prybila

> Orwell shows the pigs becoming <u>more like</u> their <u>human masters</u> — this time the pigs treat the animals <u>worse than Jones</u> did. Jones used to put some milk in the hens' mash, but the pigs <u>keep it all</u>.

So, the pigs did it — shame I've already had the butler arrested...

Orwell was keen to make his audience aware that the bit where the pigs steal the milk and apples was an important moment. He said that if the animals had stood up to the pigs early on, the outcome would have been different.

Analysis of Chapter Four — Battle of the Cowshed

Chapter Four centres around the Battle of the Cowshed. If you like blood and guts then this is the chapter for you. The animals defeat the first wave of human forces, but if I know good storytelling, they'll be back...

The **Humans** are **Worried** that the **Rebellion** will **Spread**

1) News of the farm's success spreads despite Pilkington and Frederick's attempts to stop it.

2) The pigeons teach neighbouring farms 'Beasts of England' — animals on other farms carry out small acts of disruption against their masters.

Allegory

Trotsky wanted to spread the revolution as far as possible — and so does Snowball.

The humans are presented as cruel and hypocritical — Man treats animals badly everywhere. This backs up Major's speech and justifies the revolution. This suggests that Orwell isn't anti-revolution, but against corruption of power.

The **Animals Win** the **Battle of the Cowshed**...

Allegory

Trotsky was a great strategist, who led the Russian army to many great victories (see p. 8).

1) Snowball is an excellent general — he studies Caesar's campaigns, "was in charge of the defensive operations" and "gave his orders quickly". He also knocks Jones off his feet even when he's injured.

2) Snowball leads the charge and never falters — his commitment to Animalism is so great that he's willing to sacrifice his life for the cause. Napoleon's commitment is more questionable — Orwell doesn't describe Napoleon's role in the battle, which suggests he didn't do much at all.

...but there are **Consequences**

1) Boxer's kindness is shown by his concern for the stable boy. He wants to use as little force as possible.

2) Snowball dismisses Boxer's "sentimentality", saying "the only good human being is a dead one". Boxer's feelings contrast with Napoleon's use of violence later in the novel.

3) Snowball and Boxer receive "Animal Hero, First Class" medals. The dead sheep gets "Animal Hero, Second Class".

The medals establish an inequality that didn't exist before — they're meant to inspire the animals, but they also separate them.

Rewarding Boxer's loyalty increases the pigs' control over him. It encourages other animals to be more like him — obedient and unquestioning.

4) Snowball uses the sheep's death to remind the animals that they should be loyal to the farm and be prepared to sacrifice themselves. This increases the pigs' control.

---

fight, Fight, FIGHT, FIGHT, FIGHT — sorry, got carried away there...

Snowball does have a lot of good characteristics — he's a good leader, he wants to educate everyone and he has lots of ideas about improving the farm. However, even he agreed that the pigs should keep the milk and apples — he's not perfect.

Analysis of Chapter Five — Snowball is Exiled

The pigs have now <u>completely taken control</u> of <u>the decision making process</u>, but their decisions must still be agreed by a <u>majority vote</u>. Snowball and Napoleon <u>disagree</u> every time "disagreement was possible".

Snowball's and Napoleon's Arguments Come to a Head

Snowball is Napoleon's only <u>rival</u>. The windmill debate gives Napoleon an excuse to <u>drive</u> Snowball off the farm so that he can be <u>in charge</u>:

Snowball wants to "stir up <u>rebellion</u>" on <u>other farms</u> and spread the message of <u>Animalism</u>. The humans would be <u>distracted</u> so the animals "would have no need to defend themselves".

Napoleon has more <u>violent</u> ideas. He wants to protect the farm with <u>weapons</u>.

Snowball is <u>full of ideas</u> to improve farm life and is very <u>knowledgeable</u>. He's an <u>intellectual</u> and is interested in making a "close study" of books. He's also a very <u>persuasive speaker</u>.

Napoleon undermines Snowball's ideas by <u>building support</u> among the sheep — they start bleating to <u>interrupt Snowball's speeches</u> at <u>important points</u>.

Snowball is keen to <u>build a windmill</u>. It'll be <u>hard work</u>, but could mean the animals only have to work <u>three-day weeks</u>.

Napoleon responds by <u>urinating over the windmill plans</u> — he calls them "nonsense". At the final windmill debate Napoleon orders his "<u>enormous dogs</u>" to chase Snowball from the farm.

Napoleon uses <u>threats</u> (e.g. urinating on the windmill plans) and <u>violence</u> (e.g. unleashing his attack dogs) instead of taking part in a <u>fair debate</u>. Orwell shows the reader an <u>unpleasant</u> alternative to <u>democracy</u> through Napoleon's actions, suggesting that it's important to Orwell that democracy doesn't ever <u>fail</u>.

Napoleon starts to take Absolute Control

1) Napoleon <u>cancels Sunday meetings</u> and sets up a <u>special committee of pigs</u> to make all the decisions <u>without a public vote</u>. This isn't <u>democratic</u>.

2) The other animals aren't <u>clever</u> enough to find "the right arguments" to <u>protest</u> and are scared into <u>silence</u>.

3) Squealer promotes the new regime using <u>propaganda</u>, saying that Napoleon has done everyone a favour by <u>taking on more work</u>.

Theme — Language

<u>Language is power</u>, and so Napoleon sets about ending <u>freedom of speech</u> (see p. 39).

This is the beginning of Napoleon's <u>dictatorship</u> and a sharp <u>contrast</u> with the <u>harmony</u> that came after the rebellion. The <u>more</u> like Man Napoleon becomes, the <u>less likely</u> the society will be equal.

Snowball and Napoleon's rivalry is intense — like camping...

By eliminating Snowball, Napoleon manages to remove the main threat to his rule. The other animals don't approve of Napoleon's rule, but their lack of education means they aren't really a danger. Squealer can keep them under control...

Analysis of Chapter Six — Commandments Change

Great Scott! The pigs are <u>changing the past</u>...
Napoleon decides to <u>change the rules</u> to <u>suit his purposes</u> — where we're going we don't need rules.

The pigs *Start Changing* the *Rules*

1) Napoleon introduces <u>work on Sunday afternoons</u>, which was previously a day for rest. He says it's "strictly voluntary" but if anyone refuses, their <u>rations are halved</u>.

This <u>threat</u> is <u>hidden</u> by <u>clever words</u> — the work's <u>compulsory</u>, but Napoleon calls it "<u>voluntary</u>".

2) Napoleon decides to work with Mr Whymper, a local solicitor. Napoleon claims that it's <u>not for commercial gain</u> — but there are rumours of a deal with Pilkington or Frederick.

Napoleon breaks another of <u>Major's rules</u> by allowing <u>humans</u> on the farm. <u>Capitalism</u> is back.

3) The pigs move <u>into the farmhouse</u> and start <u>sleeping in beds</u>.

The pigs continue to live <u>separately</u>, and become <u>more like Man</u>.

4) They go on to <u>change the original commandment</u> to read "No animal shall sleep in a bed *with sheets*".

<u>Animalism</u> has been <u>corrupted</u> and the pigs start to <u>abuse language</u>.

5) The pigs also decide that they need <u>more sleep</u> and get up an hour later than the others. This is simply <u>accepted</u> by the other animals.

The pigs are <u>lazy</u>. This <u>contrasts</u> with Boxer's <u>selfless hard work</u>.

Squealer Increases Fear on the farm

1) When the pigs move into the farmhouse, Squealer says this was <u>never against the rules</u> — the animals must have <u>imagined</u> it.

2) He <u>threatens the animals</u> — saying <u>Jones will come back</u> if the pigs don't get enough rest. This stops them from <u>protesting</u>.

<u>Threats</u> of Jones' <u>return</u> make the animals think that conditions are <u>better now</u> than they were <u>before</u> — they can't rely on their <u>memories</u>.

© iStockphoto.com/Steve Geer

Snowball is Used as a *Scapegoat*

A scapegoat is someone who is singled out and punished for something they haven't done.

1) When the windmill <u>collapses in the storm</u>, Napoleon screams that <u>Snowball sabotaged</u> it because he's a "miserable traitor".

2) Napoleon passes the <u>death sentence</u> on Snowball, and promises a <u>reward</u> to whoever catches him.

Using Snowball as a scapegoat is a <u>useful tactic</u>. It's one that Napoleon uses <u>many times</u> as it makes the animals <u>scared of an invisible enemy</u>, rather than focusing on Napoleon's reign of terror.

Scapegoats — always getting blamed while scapecows get off scot-free...

By this stage in the novel, all of the central themes should be clear, and the ending should be pretty obvious. The slope that the pigs have found themselves on is a slippery one, and there's no way back up it.

Analysis of Chapter Seven — The Hens Rebel

Squealer <u>makes up more lies</u> to make Snowball seem like an <u>all-powerful</u>, <u>invisible enemy</u>. Scary stuff. Forget about the monster in your closet, it's the league of evil super-pigs you should be worrying about.

More *Blame* is *Placed* on *Snowball*...

1) Conditions get <u>worse</u>. Napoleon <u>uses Snowball</u> as an <u>excuse</u> for the <u>worsening conditions</u>:

> - Snowball apparently <u>returns each night</u> — the cows are so <u>paranoid</u> they claim that Snowball milks them in their sleep.
> - <u>Squealer claims</u> that Snowball was "in <u>league with Jones</u>".

2) This imaginary threat <u>unites the farm</u> against Snowball and makes the animals question their <u>memory</u> of him. They are "thoroughly frightened" — Napoleon <u>takes advantage</u> of their <u>fear</u> to make himself more <u>popular</u>.

3) Squealer <u>rewrites history</u> by saying <u>Napoleon was behind</u> the Cowshed victory and it's described so <u>graphically</u> that the animals <u>start to remember it</u>.

> Napoleon now <u>controls</u> the animals' <u>memories</u> — it's even <u>worse</u> than controlling their actions. Orwell shows how <u>scary</u> Stalin's regime was in Russia — and he's <u>warning</u> never to let it happen again <u>anywhere else</u>.

...but *Napoleon* still has to *Deal* with *Resistance*

1) The hens are told to <u>give up their eggs</u> to be sold, but they rebel by laying their eggs from the rafters so they <u>smash on the floor</u>.

2) This is one of the <u>few times</u> the animals stand up to Napoleon. Napoleon is ruthless and <u>cuts off</u> all their <u>food</u>. Nine hens <u>die</u> before the others give in.

> **Allegory**
>
> The hens' <u>rebellion</u> echoes the <u>kulaks' resistance</u> to <u>collectivisation</u> (see p. 10).

Napoleon *Steps Up* his *Campaign* of *Terror*

1) Napoleon sets his dogs on anyone who <u>threatens him</u> — Boxer is attacked for not believing the lies about Snowball, and so are the pigs who <u>object to Napoleon's regime</u>.

> **Allegory**
>
> This satirises <u>Stalin's purges</u>.

2) Boxer defeats the dogs, but the pigs '<u>confess</u>' to working with Snowball. Napoleon <u>forces confessions</u> from many other 'traitors' and they're <u>executed</u> by the dogs.

> - Orwell describes this part from <u>Clover's point of view</u>. She <u>doesn't understand</u> how they've got to this terrible situation, but she <u>says nothing</u> — "There was no thought of rebellion or disobedience in her mind." This makes the executions seem <u>worse</u> because Clover stays <u>blindly loyal</u> to Napoleon.
> - This <u>change of perspective</u> also reminds the reader of the <u>contrast</u> between Major's original <u>utopian vision</u> that Clover remembers and Napoleon's <u>cruel dictatorship</u>.

Old Napoleon had a farm — Eek! Argh! Eek! Argh! Ouch!

Farm life seems pretty miserable in this chapter — singing 'Beasts of England' is also banned, as it's a song of rebellion and is no longer needed. Napoleon's probably frightened of a second revolution which could overthrow him.

Analysis of Chapter Eight — Battle of the Windmill

Major's speech in Chapter One made it clear that the "habits of Man" are a great evil, but the pigs have now completely embraced a human lifestyle. But, in fairness, I think I'd rather sleep in a bed than a sty...

Napoleon's Regime is now in Full Flow...

1) After the executions, the sixth commandment is changed to "No animal shall kill another animal without cause" to justify Napoleon's trials and killings.

2) Squealer continues to spread propaganda presenting Napoleon as a good leader:

- He reads out lists telling of increased productivity and profits.

- Napoleon is called "our Leader, Comrade Napoleon" and he's given credit for everything — even for how good the water tastes.

- A poem celebrating Napoleon is written opposite the commandments.

Theme — Animalism

It's as if Napoleon has become as important as the commandments.

3) Squealer's propaganda is ironic — while he claims that things are getting better, the reader can see how quickly things are getting worse.

But there's Unrest on the farm

1) The animals start to think that the farm is no better than it was under Jones, and there are rumours of plots to kill Napoleon. This fuels his paranoia.

2) Napoleon decides to sell timber to Frederick. Frederick pays for it in forged notes and then invades the farm. This shows that the humans can't be trusted — it highlights the problems with trade and capitalism.

© iStockphoto.com/Nick Pinkham

3) Frederick's men destroy the windmill, so the animals attack. It's the first time in ages that the animals work together but many are wounded or die. The animals are "weary and bleeding" after the battle and even Boxer's idealism starts to fail — it makes the reader sympathise with them and their difficult struggle.

Alcohol just makes things Worse...

1) Even though the windmill's gone, Squealer claims it was a victory and the pigs celebrate with whisky.

2) Orwell links alcohol to corruption in the novel — only the pigs drink alcohol, so it's another symbol of inequality on the farm. It's also one of the human habits that Major warned against.

3) The commandment is changed to "No animal shall drink alcohol to excess". It's ironic that the animals catch Squealer changing it, but don't realise that he's drunk. It shows their innocence.

George Orwell loves allegory so much — he once tried to marry it...

He didn't, just in case you're really confused. I made it up. But the point is, everything that happens in *Animal Farm* is pretty much an allegory of events in Russia. You just need to brush up on your history. Try Section One for starters...

Analysis of Chapter Nine — Boxer Dies

By this point in the novel, the pigs feel so <u>confident in their control</u>, they feel as if they <u>don't need to justify</u> their actions. This is the chapter where we say <u>goodbye to Boxer</u>. The pages in my book are covered with tears...

*Animalism is **Completely Corrupted***

1) Boxer's <u>hard work</u> and <u>suffering</u> contrasts with the pigs' <u>laziness</u>.

2) Squealer says a "<u>too-rigid equality in rations</u>" is "<u>contrary to the principles of Animalism</u>". This goes against Major's beliefs.

3) The pigs don't <u>justify</u> their actions — this shows how <u>deep</u> their <u>corruption</u> is because they don't feel the need to hide it:

   • Pigs are allowed to wear <u>green ribbons on Sundays</u>.

   • Animals are told to "<u>stand aside</u>" if they meet a pig on a path.

*The pigs use **New Tactics** to keep the farm **Happy***

1) Once a week there's a "<u>Spontaneous Demonstration</u>" where the animals parade around with Napoleon at the front. <u>Poems</u> and <u>songs</u> are performed <u>in Napoleon's honour</u>.

Theme — Language

The pigs <u>abuse language</u> — the parades are called "Spontaneous", but they're <u>organised</u>, and the farm's declared a "Republic", but Napoleon's a <u>dictator</u>.

2) The farm becomes a <u>Republic</u>, and it needs a President. There's only <u>one candidate</u> — Napoleon.

3) Moses returns, speaking about <u>Sugarcandy Mountain</u>. The animals <u>believe him</u>, hoping for a <u>better life</u>.

4) The animals' <u>innocent belief</u> in a better future helps to take their minds off the "harsh" farm conditions — <u>rumours</u> and <u>stories</u> promising future rewards make the farm seem more <u>tolerable</u>. The pigs are happy for Moses to stay on the farm because his stories keep the animals <u>quiet</u> and <u>obedient</u>.

*When Boxer **Dies**, the pigs only **Care About Money***

Turning point in the action
Boxer's the most loyal worker but the pigs kill him without a thought.

1) When Boxer <u>collapses</u> and is taken to be slaughtered, the animals don't <u>react</u> until it's <u>too late</u>. This is a theme which underlies the <u>entire novel</u>.

2) Squealer says Boxer's been <u>sent to hospital</u> and the animals <u>happily accept</u> Squealer's lies.

3) Napoleon uses Boxer's death to make the other animals as <u>obedient</u> and <u>loyal as Boxer was</u>. Ironically, Boxer's <u>self sacrifice</u> and blind <u>commitment</u> to Animalism ultimately led to his death.

4) The pigs <u>buy more whisky</u> with the money from selling Boxer. They have become <u>drunks like Jones</u> and the fact that they <u>spend</u> the money from Boxer shows that they're just as <u>ruthless</u> too.

Power corrupts — but absolute power corrupts absolutely...

Squealer's propaganda is so convincing that by this point the animals actually believe that Snowball was openly fighting for Jones at the Battle of the Cowshed, and the wounds on his back were inflicted by Napoleon. Liar, liar, pants on fire.

Analysis of Chapter Ten — Animalism is Over

Chapter Ten is where you get an eerie sense of déjà vu. Orwell's point is that under Napoleon, and Stalin, the working class found themselves in the same, or worse situation that they had been in before.

Nobody *Remembers Life Before Napoleon*

1) Napoleon's power becomes <u>so great</u> that he doesn't need to use <u>scapegoats</u> or <u>fear</u> — he's not even trying to <u>hide</u> his <u>totalitarian</u> regime.

2) New animals are brought up to obey Napoleon's <u>changed commandments</u>.

3) They just <u>accept what they're told</u>, having had <u>no education</u>. This doesn't bode well for the <u>future</u>, as there's even <u>less chance</u> that the pigs will be overthrown.

Theme — Education
An <u>uneducated</u> working class are unlikely to <u>rise up</u> against their leaders.

The *Pigs Profit* while the *Others Suffer*

1) The farm is <u>rich</u>, but the animals work harder than ever. Napoleon tells them that Animalism means "<u>working hard</u>" and "<u>living frugally</u>".

2) The farm may have more <u>money</u>, but only the <u>pigs</u> and <u>dogs benefit</u>.

3) The animals feel "<u>honour</u> and <u>privilege</u>" that the farm is <u>run by animals</u>. It's ironic because they truly believe that they <u>work for themselves</u> and <u>hope</u> that a "<u>Republic of Animals</u>" will still form. All the <u>evidence</u> suggests this isn't true, but the animals have been <u>brainwashed</u> into believing it.

4) The original <u>commandments are rubbed out</u>, and replaced with one commandment — "<u>ALL ANIMALS ARE EQUAL BUT SOME ARE MORE EQUAL THAN OTHERS</u>". The fact that this statement doesn't even <u>make sense</u> shows how much Napoleon has <u>corrupted language</u> and how his <u>power</u> over the other animals is <u>absolute</u>.

Theme — Animalism
When Animalism was <u>founded</u> it meant <u>equality</u> and <u>freedom</u>. Napoleon <u>completely changes</u> it.

Pig *or* Human — *it's Impossible To Tell*

1) The pigs <u>carry whips</u> and <u>wear clothes</u> — they're acting like <u>humans</u>.

Turning point in the action
The revolution has come full circle — the animals are back where they started.

© HALLMARK/TNT/ANIMAL FARM PRODUCTION
COURTESY THE KOBAL COLLECTION

2) Napoleon removes anything related to Animalism:

- He's going to <u>stop the animals</u> calling each other "Comrade" as it <u>shows equality</u>.

- He tries to <u>erase memories</u> of Major and <u>what he stood for</u> by burying his skull.

- He replaces the <u>symbolic Animalism</u> flag.

3) Animal Farm <u>becomes</u> Manor Farm again, in <u>more than just name</u> — pigs and men now <u>look the same</u>.

4) Napoleon is a <u>tyrant</u> like Jones — except that the pigs treat the animals even <u>worse</u> than Jones did. This shows that the revolution has ultimately achieved <u>nothing</u>.

Ground control to Major Pig — there's something wrong...

The tyrant Napoleon, with his vicious loyal dogs in tow, has created a more efficient, brutal version of Jones' Manor Farm for the sole benefit of the pigs themselves. The other animals are no more than slaves.

Practice Questions

These questions are meant to help you learn. Makes sense. They don't call me Mr Sensible for nothing.
Remember, these aren't exam questions, these are just helpful ways to remind yourself of the main plot points.
Anyways — as soon as I've put on my sunglasses, tutu and flippers, I'm off for a tea break. Mr Sensible out.

Quick Questions

Q1   What does old Major teach the animals during his speech?

Q2   Give one example of an issue that Snowball and Napoleon disagree on.

Q3   At first how does Napoleon feel about Snowball's windmill plan?
        How does he show this?

Q4   How do the animals react to Snowball's expulsion from the farm?

Q5   How does Squealer promote Napoleon's new regime?

Q6   How does Napoleon justify trading with humans?

Q7   How does Napoleon deal with the hens' resistance?

Q8   Give two examples of how the pigs start to be treated better under Napoleon's regime.

Q9   Briefly explain why the other animals can't tell the difference
        between the humans and the pigs at the end of the novel.

In-depth Questions

Q1   Briefly explain why the 'milk and apples' incident is a key turning point in the novel.

Q2   How do the medals awarded after the 'Battle of the Cowshed' undermine Animalism?

Q3   Briefly explain the purpose of Napoleon's trials and executions.

Q4   Why do the pigs allow Moses to stay on the farm?

Character Profile — Napoleon

Napoleon is the <u>villain</u> of the book. He doesn't have many redeeming qualities, so it's <u>difficult</u> to like or <u>sympathise</u> with him. Unless you're a totalitarian dictator...

Napoleon doesn't Fight in the Revolution

1) Napoleon <u>doesn't say much</u> in the early meetings, but he has a "reputation" for getting what he wants. This shows that he seems to care less about Animalism than the others, and hints that he's <u>ambitious</u> and <u>selfish</u>.

2) At the Battle of the Cowshed he disappears — he's a <u>coward</u>. This contrasts with Snowball who fights <u>bravely</u> to defend the farm.

© iStockphoto.com/Uros Petrovic

> **Napoleon is...**
>
> **cunning:** "That, he said, was Comrade Napoleon's cunning"
> **ruthless:** "a pile of corpses lying before Napoleon's feet"
> **corrupt:** "There was only one candidate, Napoleon"
> **selfish:** "reputation for getting his own way"

He's a Ruthless character

Napoleon doesn't care about the <u>welfare</u> of the other animals and just <u>uses</u> them for his own <u>benefit</u>:

- He adopts the puppies, but only so that he can train them to be his <u>army</u>.
- He forces the animals to work a <u>60-hour week</u> while he does <u>nothing</u>.
- He <u>steals</u> the apples and cows' milk for the pigs to have for themselves.

> **Allegory**
>
> Napoleon is based on <u>Joseph Stalin</u>, the <u>leader</u> of Soviet Russia (see p. 9).

Napoleon uses Cunning and Brutality to get his own way

1) Napoleon is <u>threatened</u> by Snowball, who is a military hero and a charismatic leader.

2) Napoleon <u>belittles</u> and <u>undermines</u> Snowball. He trains the sheep to <u>interrupt</u> Snowball's speeches and <u>urinates</u> on his plans for the windmill. He then uses his army of dogs to chase Snowball into <u>exile</u>.

3) After his exile, Napoleon uses Snowball as a <u>scapegoat</u> for any problems on the farm. The way that he turns the animals <u>against</u> Snowball is <u>cunning</u>.

4) He uses <u>terror</u> to <u>control</u> the farm. Animals are forced to make <u>false confessions</u> and are <u>executed</u> for being in league with Snowball.

> **Allegory**
>
> The executions and show trials (see p. 10) mimic the <u>brutality</u> of Stalin in the 1930s. Many Russians were <u>executed</u> or sent to <u>labour camps</u>.

Character Profile — Napoleon

Napoleon emerges as the <u>leader</u> of Animal Farm after using some <u>filthy</u> tactics. He's become a paranoid, brutal tyrant who's drunk on <u>power</u> (and probably whisky). It's time for the bacon to bite back...

*Napoleon is a **Selfish Leader**...*

1) Napoleon sees himself as <u>better</u> than the other animals and above the common herd.

2) He changes the principles of Animalism for his own <u>benefit</u>, e.g. "No animal shall drink alcohol *to excess*." It shows that he <u>quickly forgets</u> any ideals of Animalism that he may have believed in.

3) Although he <u>criticises</u> Snowball's plans for the windmill, he builds it after Snowball's exile. He's happy to take the <u>credit</u> for someone else's ideas.

© iStockphoto.com/Peter Dean

*...and a **Corrupt Ruler***

Theme — Education

The animals have <u>doubts</u> about Napoleon but they don't question him — they have been brainwashed into thinking that "Napoleon is always right".

1) Napoleon rewrites history — he <u>distorts</u> the story of the Battle of the Cowshed to make himself seem like a hero. He awards himself a bravery medal and presents Snowball as a <u>traitor</u>.

2) The Sunday meetings are <u>abolished</u> to <u>suppress</u> debate and <u>criticism</u> towards him.

3) He is "unanimously" elected as the leader of the Republic but he is the <u>only</u> candidate.

Theme — Propaganda

Just like Napoleon, Stalin created a <u>cult of personality</u>, where propaganda and the media were used to <u>glorify</u> him as a kind, caring leader (see p.9).

*He's just as **Bad** as **Farmer Jones***

1) Napoleon's transition from pig to '<u>human</u>' is complete by the end of the novel — he stands on two legs, drinks whisky, and wears clothes. When the animals look at the pigs and men, they can't say "<u>which was which</u>".

2) By the end, the commandments and principles of Animalism have been <u>forgotten</u> — the animals are <u>starving</u> and <u>overworked</u> and in a worse position than they were under Farmer Jones.

Theme — Class System

Animalism <u>failed</u> because one <u>tyrant</u>, Farmer Jones, was replaced with another, Napoleon. This reflects the way that the all-powerful Tsar was <u>replaced</u> by Stalin and his dictatorship.

Animal Farm — it's piggin' clever...

Although Napoleon is an allegory of Stalin, and the namesake of a tyrannical French leader, Orwell wanted the reader to realise that a lot of what happens in *Animal Farm*, especially the <u>corruption</u> of power, could be applied elsewhere.

Character Profile — Snowball

Snowball isn't exactly <u>villainous</u>, but it doesn't mean he has a <u>happy ending</u>. He's a smart, idealistic character who wants Animalism to <u>succeed</u> and believes in the equality of animals.

Snowball is Intelligent but not very Cunning

1) Snowball is <u>lively</u> and a <u>quick thinker</u>, but he doesn't have "the same depth of character" as Napoleon.

2) Animal <u>equality</u> and the '<u>working class</u>' animals are important to him. He explains the principles of Animalism for the others so that they can improve life on Animal Farm.

3) He is an <u>original thinker</u> — he explains to the birds that a wing "is an organ of propulsion." He's got <u>good</u> intentions, but the birds don't <u>understand</u> Snowball's complicated explanations.

> **Allegory**
>
> Snowball's character is based on <u>Leon Trotsky</u>, the Russian revolutionary leader and Stalin's greatest <u>rival</u> (see p. 8).

4) Snowball <u>isn't perfect</u> though:

- He's <u>over-idealistic</u> — he forms animal committees but generally these end in failure.

- He's <u>dishonest</u> — when Napoleon steals the milk for the pigs, Snowball doesn't protest.

He's Brave and a Strong Military Leader

1) Snowball is a <u>strong leader</u> in battle. He's in charge of defensive operations on Animal Farm. When Jones and his allies attack, Snowball has <u>prepared</u> by studying the campaigns of Caesar.

2) He's <u>noble</u>. He leads the charge against the humans and is <u>injured</u>. He proves he's <u>willing to die</u> for Animalism.

3) For his bravery he is recognised as a <u>hero</u> by all the animals, and awarded the military <u>honour</u>, 'Animal Hero, First Class', for his role in the <u>Battle of the Cowshed</u>.

> **Snowball is...**
>
> **intelligent:** "full of plans for innovations and improvements"
> **brave:** "He himself dashed straight for Jones"
> **eloquent:** "won over the majority by his brilliant speeches"
> **idealistic:** "Snowball conjured up pictures of fantastic machines"

He wants Animalism to Succeed

A utopia is a perfect community or society.

© iStockphoto.com/chelovek

1) Snowball wants Major's utopian vision to become a <u>reality</u>.

2) He writes the seven commandments on the barn wall for all the animals to see, but most of the animals are <u>illiterate</u>.

3) He draws up <u>plans</u> for the windmill — a project designed to generate electricity for the farm to make the animals' lives <u>easier</u>.

4) His plan would require the animals to work hard but the windmill would benefit <u>everyone</u>.

Character Profile — Snowball

After the rebellion, Snowball and Napoleon become <u>leaders</u> of Animal Farm, but Napoleon isn't willing to <u>share</u> power. Snowball's intelligence and idealism prove no match for Napoleon's <u>cunning</u> and <u>brutality</u>.

Snowball is Undermined by Napoleon

1) They can't <u>agree</u> — Snowball wants to encourage <u>all</u> animals on <u>all</u> farms to rebel, but Napoleon wants to build up <u>power</u> and <u>security</u> on Animal Farm.

Turning point in the action
Once Snowball has been exiled, Napoleon can start his campaign of terror.

2) Snowball is an <u>excellent speaker</u> but Napoleon is better at "canvassing support for himself" outside the debates.

3) Napoleon is threatened by Snowball's <u>heroism</u>, <u>intelligence</u> and <u>influence</u> over the other animals, and so he begins to <u>bully</u> him:

- Napoleon trains the sheep to <u>disrupt</u> Snowball's speeches.

- When Snowball draws up the windmill plans, Napoleon shows his <u>contempt</u> by <u>urinating</u> all over them.

- Snowball is <u>chased</u> off the farm by Napoleon's dogs.

He becomes a Scapegoat

A scapegoat is someone who is singled out and blamed for something they haven't done.

1) After Snowball is exiled from Animal Farm, Napoleon begins to gain <u>power</u>. He spreads vicious rumours and lies about the threat of Snowball to <u>safeguard</u> his own position.

© iStockphoto.com/chelovek

2) Snowball is condemned as a <u>traitor</u>, a <u>liar</u> and a friend of Farmer Jones.

3) He becomes a <u>scapegoat</u> — when the windmill is blown down in a storm, Snowball is <u>blamed</u>. He becomes the "source of all evil" on the farm.

4) Napoleon denounces Snowball as a dangerous outside enemy, and puts himself forward as the <u>protector</u> of Animal Farm.

Allegory

When Stalin came to power, he ordered Trotsky and other political rivals to be <u>exiled</u>. He then began to <u>persecute</u> people who supported or sympathised with Trotsky (see p. 10).

It all just snowballed out of control...

Poor Snowball, he had such good intentions. He's very nearly the hero of the story, but unfortunately for him, the typical hero's fate of girls, gold and glory doesn't work out. It's true what they say — nice pigs always finish last.

Character Profile — Squealer

Squealer is a piggy <u>spin doctor</u> — he's used by Napoleon to <u>influence</u> and <u>persuade</u> the other animals by any means. He <u>rewrites</u> history, <u>distorts</u> the facts and gives a whole new meaning to 'telling a porkie'.

Squealer is a Remorseless Liar

1) Squealer is a small, fat porker with "twinkling eyes" and a "shrill <u>voice</u>".

2) He spends the novel <u>promoting</u> Napoleon's regime — <u>distorting language</u> and <u>telling</u> lies.

3) He's <u>protected</u> by vicious dogs, who <u>scare</u> the other animals into <u>silence</u>.

Allegory

Squealer represents the use of <u>communist propaganda</u> in Russia — the working classes were controlled by <u>persuasive slogans</u> (see p. 40).

© iStockphoto.com/Chris Hepburn

Squealer is...

persuasive: "he had a way of skipping from side to side and whisking his tail which was somehow very persuasive"

manipulative: "he could turn black into white"

deceitful: Squealer says that "Snowball was in league with Jones"

He uses Persuasive Language to Justify Napoleon's actions

1) When Napoleon is the leader of Animal Farm, Squealer becomes his loyal <u>spokesperson</u>.

2) He uses convincing language to <u>win</u> over the other animals. He tells them that, "No one believes more firmly than Napoleon" in the equality of animals.

3) He <u>manipulates</u> the animals' fear of Jones in order to increase Napoleon's power. He asks them, "you do not want Jones back?" to make it seem like they only have a <u>choice</u> between the <u>two</u>.

4) Squealer has an <u>answer</u> for everything. When all the animals have their rations reduced except the pigs and dogs, Squealer explains that rigid equality is "contrary" to Animalism.

Theme — Education

<u>Propaganda</u> is used as a tool by the pigs to <u>control</u> the other animals and <u>justify</u> unequal living conditions. The use of statistics and jargon <u>confuses</u> the poorly educated animals (see p. 38).

Squealer Controls the animals with Lies

Squealer <u>manipulates</u> the animals through his <u>clever</u> use of language, <u>distorting</u> the truth to convince them that life is <u>better</u> on Animal Farm.

- He uses <u>false statistics</u> to claim that life is good on the farm: he "proved" to the animals in detail that they had more food than before the Rebellion.

- Squealer <u>lies</u> — he claims that the Battle of the Windmill was a great victory — even though the animals suffered terrible losses and the windmill was destroyed.

- He <u>rewrites</u> history. He turns Napoleon into the hero at the Battle of the Cowshed by saying things like "Comrade Napoleon sprang forward... and sank his teeth into Jones's leg".

Character Profile — Squealer

Not only is Squealer a master of persuasion, he's also a <u>nasty</u> piece of work. He creates a smear campaign against Snowball, ruining his reputation, and he lies about Boxer's death. He's just as <u>vicious</u> as Napoleon.

*Squealer **Turns** the animals **Against Snowball***

1) Squealer plays an important role in <u>destroying</u> Snowball's reputation and turning the other animals against him.

2) When he suggests that Snowball's agents are "lurking among us at this moment", he's <u>scaremongering</u>.

3) He <u>makes up evidence</u> against Snowball. He says Snowball was "Jones's secret agent" and it's been "proved by documents".

4) He <u>convinces</u> the animals that Snowball was a <u>traitor</u> at the Battle of the Cowshed and that Snowball was never awarded 'Animal Hero, First Class'.

Theme — Language

Orwell uses Squealer to show how <u>language</u> can be used to <u>influence</u> people. Squealer's ability to <u>twist</u> language gives him great <u>power</u> — and this kind of subtle control is <u>dangerous</u>.

*He **Lies** about Boxer's **Death***

1) The ageing Boxer is <u>betrayed</u> and sold to the knacker's yard to be killed.

2) Squealer's <u>lies</u> about the death of Boxer are more <u>fanciful</u> than ever.

3) He describes Boxer's death in great sentimental detail, even though it's completely <u>made up</u>. He claims that Boxer's last words were, "Napoleon is always right". This shows that he is completely <u>remorseless</u>, willing to <u>abuse</u> Boxer's unfailing loyalty to Napoleon to the end.

4) He says that Napoleon did <u>all he could</u> for Boxer, providing medicine "without a thought as to the cost". This is <u>ironic</u> because Napoleon's only real <u>concern</u> was how much <u>money</u> the pigs could make by <u>selling</u> Boxer.

Theme — Propaganda

Stalin was given the titles 'Papa Stalin' and 'Little Father of the Peoples'. He was often depicted embracing children in propaganda posters — in an attempt to show that he was a <u>caring</u>, <u>loving</u> leader (see p. 40).

*Squealer helps to **Create** and **Maintain** the **Dictatorship***

Squealer is a very important member of Napoleon's regime:

- He helps to build up Napoleon's <u>oppressive</u>, <u>murderous</u> dictatorship.

- With Squealer's help, Animal Farm becomes a more efficient <u>state of terror</u>.

- It's a new <u>class-based hierarchy</u> where the interests of the pigs are put first.

A Russian propaganda poster which says "To our beloved Stalin, the nation's happiness"

This little piggy went to market, this little piggy lied his face off...

Squealer is a symbol of Stalin's use of Russian propaganda. Squealer goes about influencing the uneducated working classes with memorable slogans, distorted facts and persuasive language. Revision is fun, Comrades!

Character Profile — Old Major and Benjamin

Old Major dreams of a better <u>future</u> for the animals. He thinks that without Man, they'll all be happy clappy together. Benjamin thinks everything will stay the same. No guesses as to whose glass is half full then...

Old Major has a **Vision**

1) Old Major is the <u>oldest</u>, <u>wisest</u> pig on the farm.

2) He dreams of a future where all animals live in a land of <u>happiness</u> and <u>plenty</u>, free from the exploitation of man.

3) He's aware that he's near death and has a clear <u>mission</u> to pass on his wisdom.

Old Major is...

> **kindly:** "with a wise and benevolent appearance"
>
> **wise:** "to pass on to you such wisdom as I have acquired"
>
> **idealistic:** "let there be perfect unity, perfect comradeship"

Allegory

> Old Major is the equivalent of <u>Karl Marx</u> and Russian revolutionary, <u>Vladimir Lenin</u> (see p. 6-7).

© iStockphoto.com/Nancy Nehring

His **Ideas** *for the* **Future** *are* **Clear**

1) When old Major gives his speech, he talks about Man's <u>terrible treatment</u> of animals. He says, "our lives are miserable, laborious and short".

2) Old Major's vision becomes the foundation of <u>Animalism</u>:

Even though old Major complains about Man, he's had a long, healthy life on Manor Farm.

- He insists that all animals are "<u>comrades</u>" — they are all <u>equal</u>.
- Man is the <u>enemy</u> and animals must never come to resemble him.
- Before his death he sets out a number of <u>clear rules</u> against adopting <u>human vices</u> such as living in houses, sleeping in beds, wearing clothes and drinking alcohol.

Unlike Major, **Benjamin** *is* **Cynical**

1) Benjamin is a <u>grumpy</u>, <u>bad-tempered</u> donkey who never laughs because "he saw nothing to laugh at". He's <u>cynical</u> about the rebellion and Animalism.

2) He's very <u>intelligent</u>, and one of the few <u>literate</u> animals but he sees little point in using his abilities.

Allegory

> Benjamin represents the <u>intellectual</u> Russians (intelligentsia) who realise that communism will not solve the <u>injustices</u> of society.

3) Benjamin has a true <u>understanding</u> of life on Animal Farm. He's <u>realistic</u> when he sees "hardship and disappointment" all around him, but he doesn't do <u>anything</u> to stop the pigs. This could suggest that Orwell is <u>disappointed</u> that many people seem <u>unwilling</u> or <u>unable</u> to <u>challenge</u> a tyrannical leader.

4) When he <u>realises</u> what's happening to Boxer, he raises the alarm. This is an important turning point for Benjamin — it's the first time that he <u>speaks out</u> but he reacts <u>too late</u>.

Old Major is the piggy in the middle...

One of the first things Napoleon does as leader is to put Major's skull on display. It makes the animals think that he's been inspired by Major's ideas, but this is just an illusion — Napoleon doesn't care about Major's dream.

Character Profile — Boxer

Boxer is a loyal, simple and hardworking cart-horse — his labour is <u>important</u> to the farm's initial success. He is <u>devoted</u> to Animalism but blindly follows the leaders without thinking for <u>himself</u>.

Boxer is Brave and Hardworking

1) Boxer is the <u>hardest worker</u> on the farm — all the farm's work seemed "to rest upon his mighty shoulders".

2) He is as <u>strong</u> "as any two horses put together".

3) At the Battle of the Cowshed he fights <u>bravely</u> and is awarded 'Animal Hero, First Class'.

4) The animals <u>respect</u> Boxer for his calm, stable manner and his tremendous ability to work.

5) Boxer gets <u>upset</u> when he thinks he's <u>killed</u> a human boy during the Battle of the Cowshed. This shows that he's <u>compassionate</u>.

© iStockphoto.com/Russell Du parcq

He Trusts the Pigs Completely

Boxer is...

loyal: "Napoleon is always right"
hardworking: "I must work harder"
dim-witted: "not of first-rate intelligence"

1) Boxer isn't very <u>bright</u> and he's <u>easily manipulated</u> by the pigs.

2) After Napoleon's show trials and executions, Boxer has <u>misgivings</u> about the pigs' behaviour but he remains silent — continuing to believe in Napoleon.

3) He's a <u>useful tool</u> for the pigs — if Boxer's on their <u>side</u> then the other animals may <u>follow</u> more easily.

Boxer's <u>dedication</u> to the farm is ultimately his <u>downfall</u>. Every time he witnesses a terrible event on the farm, he just works <u>harder</u>. He overworks himself for the good of the farm.

Boxer is Betrayed by Napoleon

1) After the Battle of the Windmill, Boxer is injured but he <u>refuses</u> to lighten his load. He's <u>determined</u> to build the windmill, however hard it is.

2) When he <u>collapses</u> and is taken ill, he believes that he will get a happy <u>retirement</u>.

3) He thinks he is being sent to the vet for treatment but Napoleon <u>sells</u> him to the <u>knacker's yard</u> so that the pigs can get money for whisky.

Allegory

Boxer represents the <u>Russian working class</u> who worked hard in appalling conditions to try to achieve the unattainable goals set by the government, for no reward.

Encouraging revision is like flogging a dead horse...

Too soon? Boxer is a staunch supporter of Animalism and devotes his life to working hard for the cause, but he's betrayed by the pigs in a horrific way. Benjamin realises that Boxer's been set up, but it's too late to save his bacon...

Character Profile — Clover and Mollie

Clover is a <u>loyal</u> follower of Animalism, but Mollie <u>couldn't care less</u>.
They're pretty much opposites — here are the details, straight from the horse's mouth...

Clover is a Mother Figure

1) She is a <u>compassionate</u>, <u>maternal</u> mare. When the animals were frightened, they "huddled about Clover".

2) She is a <u>loyal</u> and <u>faithful</u> disciple of Animalism, absorbing and passing on all that she is taught. When she grows suspicious of the pigs' behaviour, she <u>blames herself</u> for <u>misremembering</u> the commandments.

3) Even when Animalism <u>disappoints</u> her, "these scenes of terror and slaughter were not what they had looked forward to", she continues to be <u>obedient</u> and <u>accepts</u> Napoleon's leadership.

© iStockphoto.com/Sylwia Kachel

Clover is...

loyal: "she would remain faithful"
maternal: "stout motherly mare"
dim: she "could not put words together"

Theme —Education

Like Boxer, Clover represents the <u>unquestioning</u> working classes. She sometimes doubts the motives of Napoleon, but she doesn't think she's <u>intelligent</u> enough to speak out.

Mollie is Vain and Silly

1) Mollie's a "pretty white mare" who's <u>vain</u> and "<u>foolish</u>".

2) She is <u>spoiled</u> and likes ribbons, sugar and being petted — things which are <u>banned</u> under Animalism.

3) She has no interest in <u>politics</u> or the <u>rebellion</u>. She's <u>cowardly</u> and unwilling to fight for Animal Farm. She hides in fear during the Battle of the Cowshed.

Mollie is...

vain: "foolishly gazing at her own reflection"
lazy: "She was late for work every morning"
cowardly: "she was found hiding in her stall"

She refuses to make Sacrifices after the Revolution

Allegory

Mollie could represent the <u>upper-class Russians</u> who had a <u>comfortable life</u> under the Tsar (see p. 6).

1) Mollie <u>struggles</u> to follow the principles of Animalism and hoards ribbons and lump sugar. In a selfish way she's not willing to make <u>sacrifices</u>.

2) When Snowball teaches the animals to read and write, Mollie has the capacity to become literate but she only learns the letters which spell her name. She isn't interested in what the rebellion can <u>teach</u> her.

3) Mollie can't adapt to life on Animal Farm — she's too <u>shallow</u> and devoted to her <u>luxuries</u>. She runs away to draw the cart of a man who pets her and feeds her sugar.

Mollie's a bit of a dark horse...

Although Mollie's not in *Animal Farm* much, you can make some quite good points about her and how she's selfish like the pigs. Mentioning relevant bits about minor characters will really impress the examiner.

Character Profile — The Humans

The animals think they're getting a fresh Tsar-t after they <u>overthrow</u> Farmer Jones, but those pesky humans keep <u>meddling</u> in the animals' affairs, attacking the farm, ripping them off and blowing up the windmill.

Jones' *Neglect* causes the animals to *Rebel*

Allegory

Jones represents the unpopular <u>Tsar Nicholas II</u> (see p. 6).

1) Mr Jones is the owner of Manor Farm. He's a <u>lazy drunkard</u>.

2) His men are "idle", "dishonest" and they take advantage of Jones's slackness. Under Jones, the fields of Manor Farm are "full of weeds" and the animals are "underfed".

3) Jones' <u>neglect</u> and <u>drunkenness</u> allow the animals to meet and <u>organise</u> themselves in secret — he was "too drunk to remember" to lock them up properly.

4) When the animals rebel, it's a <u>spontaneous</u> event and even the animals are <u>surprised</u> by their success. This shows how little <u>control</u> Jones has over his farm.

Pilkington and *Frederick Represent* the *West*

1) Pilkington is an old-fashioned gentleman-farmer whose farm is <u>shabby</u> and <u>neglected</u>.

2) Frederick has a smaller, better kept farm. He's "tough", "shrewd" and always "involved in lawsuits." There are rumours about <u>cruelty</u> on his farm.

The Humans are...

cruel: Jones is a "hard master"

violent: "any animal caught singing it [Beasts of England] was given a flogging".

dishonest: Frederick's "bank-notes were forgeries"

Allegory

Pilkington represents the <u>capitalist West</u>. Frederick represents <u>Hitler</u> and <u>Nazi Germany</u> (see p. 10).

3) Frederick leads a surprise <u>attack</u> on Animal Farm which is <u>sudden</u> and <u>vicious</u>. He almost overthrows the animals and is only driven off after the animals suffer terrible losses and the windmill is blown up.

Whymper is in it for the *Money*

Allegory

Whymper stands for those people who were happy to work for the <u>communists</u> in Soviet Russia or do business with them, if the <u>price was right</u>.

1) Whymper is Napoleon's <u>solicitor</u> and <u>representative</u> in his dealings with other humans.

2) Whymper is a "sharp" <u>businessman</u> who realises that Napoleon's business "would be worth having".

3) He only agrees to work for Animal Farm because Napoleon tricks him into thinking the farm is <u>prosperous</u>.

Jones rules over Man-or Farm...

The humans in *Animal Farm* aren't represented favourably — they're a bunch of neglectful, unscrupulous, money-grubbing drunkards with a whiff of Nazi about them. Wonder if Orwell is trying to tell us something.

Character Profile — The Sheep, Hens and Moses

Cute, cuddly sheep, loved by small children the world over. These sheep are <u>baaaaaaaa-d</u> to the bone, but they'd still make a delicious lamb chop, with a side of Commumint sauce. <u>Delicious</u>.

The Sheep can't Think for Themselves

© iStockphoto.com/Leslie Morris

1) The sheep live up to their traditional stereotype — the members of the <u>flock</u> are <u>unthinking</u> and <u>easily led</u>.

2) They can't think for themselves and blindly <u>follow</u> the pigs' orders. They start <u>chanting</u> whenever anyone threatens to voice an <u>opinion</u> — "their usual bleating... put an end to the discussion."

3) In the end, the sheep silence all <u>opposition</u> and announce the final <u>betrayal</u> of Animalism, chanting "<u>Four legs good, two legs better!</u>"

Allegory

The sheep are like the Communist party <u>'yes-men'</u> that Stalin packed meetings with, and who would <u>vote together</u> for whatever he asked.

The Hens are Oppressed by Napoleon

1) Once he's in power, Napoleon orders the hens to give up their eggs so they can be <u>sold</u>. Trading with humans was something Major <u>opposed</u> in his speech.

Allegory

The hens are like the <u>peasants</u> of the Soviet Union who were <u>forced</u> to give up their produce. Millions of Soviet peasants <u>died</u> of famine in the 1930s (see p. 10).

2) When they're told to supply <u>400 eggs</u> a week, they protest by telling Napoleon that it is "murder."

3) They're the only group of animals to really <u>oppose</u> Napoleon's regime. When they stage a protest, Napoleon <u>starves</u> them into <u>submission</u>.

4) When egg quotas are raised again, there's no outcry or protest this time — they're too <u>frightened</u> to even raise their voices.

Moses stands for Religion

1) Moses is a raven who tells the animals stories of <u>Sugarcandy Mountain</u> — a paradise where animals go when they die.

2) He tells lies and is described as a "spy" but many of the animals <u>believe</u> him because they have nothing else to look forward to.

3) The pigs allow Moses to <u>stay</u> on Animal Farm because his stories give the animals <u>hope</u> and keep them <u>obedient</u>.

Allegory

Orwell uses Moses to introduce Karl Marx's idea that <u>religion</u> is the 'opium of the people' — he thought that religion deceived people into believing in a happy afterlife. Moses' name links the raven to the <u>Biblical prophet</u> who told of a faraway 'promised land'.

What do you call a sheep on a trampoline — a woolly jumper...

Ahahahahaha. Sorry. Those poor hens, I bet they're cursing those pesky pigs, stealing all their eggs. But you know what they always say, you've got to break a few eggs if you want to make a totalitarian, exploitative dictatorship.

Practice Questions

Animal Farm is chock-a-block with ruthless, brutal, unscrupulous characters — all the nice ones get chased away by vicious dogs, sold to glue factories or live a life of toil and starvation. Doesn't it make you feel all warm and fuzzy inside? Regardless of whether the characters are heroes or villains you still need to know what they're like, so here are some questions to warm you up for the main event.

Quick Questions

Q1   Which of the following best describes Farmer Jones at the beginning of the story?
a) drunken   b) lazy   c) neglectful   d) all of these things?

Q2   Who calls the animals to a meeting in the big barn at the beginning of the novel?
Describe his appearance and character in a few words.

Q3   Whose motto is "I will work harder"? What happens to him?

Q4   Who tricks Napoleon and nearly destroys Animal Farm in Chapter 8?

Q5   Which event in the novel is the only one to make Benjamin upset?

In-depth Questions

Q1   Describe Napoleon's personality up to the end of Chapter 3.

Q2   Snowball is portrayed as intelligent, inventive and popular, but he doesn't have the "same depth of character" as Napoleon. How does this impression of Snowball prepare you for what happens later?

Q3   Explain the animals' mixed feelings about Moses and why is he is tolerated later on in *Animal Farm*?

Q4   Why doesn't Mollie work hard for the revolution?

Q5   Who do you think is the cleverest of the pigs? Use examples to back up your answer.

Q6   Why do you think Benjamin is so cynical and grumpy? Is his attitude justified?

Q7   Explain Whymper's role. How useful is he to Napoleon?

Practice Questions

Time to break out the big guns — a set of exam-style questions to test how well you really know the book. Don't try to answer all the exam-style questions in one go — it'll make your head explode. Instead pick one, do a plan and try and write a full essay under exam conditions. Then have a break and try the next one later. Try to answer them without flicking back through these pages for hints.

Exam-Style Questions

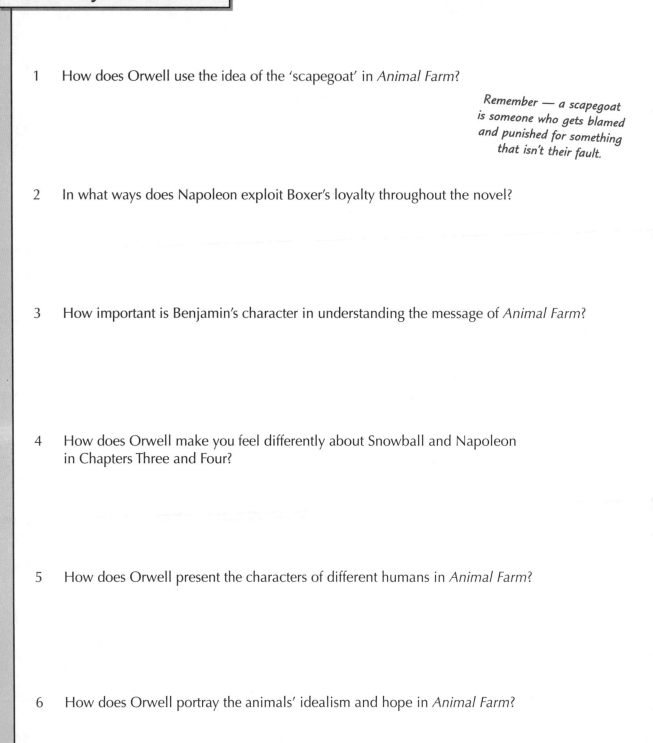

1   How does Orwell use the idea of the 'scapegoat' in *Animal Farm*?

Remember — a scapegoat is someone who gets blamed and punished for something that isn't their fault.

2   In what ways does Napoleon exploit Boxer's loyalty throughout the novel?

3   How important is Benjamin's character in understanding the message of *Animal Farm*?

4   How does Orwell make you feel differently about Snowball and Napoleon in Chapters Three and Four?

5   How does Orwell present the characters of different humans in *Animal Farm*?

6   How does Orwell portray the animals' idealism and hope in *Animal Farm*?

Animalism

Words ending in 'ism' often describe beliefs about how to live your life. Communists believe in communism and magnets believe in... er... magnetism. Animalism is how the animals believe they should live their lives.

Animalism *is the idea that animals will* **Only Work** *for* **Themselves**

1) Animalism is a new "system of thought" inspired by old Major's ideas — his beliefs are summarised in seven commandments after he dies.

2) Like communism, equality is essential in Animalism. The commandment that "All animals are equal" means that every animal should be treated the same.

3) Orwell uses the word 'commandments' to draw a comparison with the Ten Commandments of Christianity. The seven commandments are an "unalterable law" — a set of rules that the animals could follow religiously.

4) They also give the reader a framework to see Animalism's decline as the commandments are corrupted one by one.

This is the flag of the Soviet Union. The crossed horn and hoof on the Animalism flag (see p. 50) looks a bit like this.

© iStockphoto.com/Matt Trommer

> Orwell uses Animalism to represent communism so that he can criticise it indirectly. This is why the flags of both beliefs are so similar.

The **Ideals** of **Animalism** don't last long...

Not long after the revolution, there are already serious problems — and they only get worse. As the pigs corrupt Animalism, conflict and inequality increase on the farm:

Conflict

- Like Stalin, Napoleon gets rid of any opposition — he orders "nine enormous dogs" to attack Snowball and chase him from the farm. By preventing Snowball from having an equal say, Napoleon turns his back on equality and Animalism.

- Napoleon holds false trials and executes any animals who "confess" to going against Animalism. This goes against the commandment that "No animal shall kill any other animal". Ironically it's Napoleon who is actually going against Animalism by breaking one of the seven rules.

Inequality

- Some of the animals learn to read (e.g. the pigs) and so the other animals are at a disadvantage. Napoleon refuses to educate the other animals equally, so that he can maintain the pigs' authority.

- Animalism was founded on the idea that every animal worked for each other, but in reality, only the pigs benefit — they take more for themselves while the other "animals worked like slaves".

1) Power corrupts Animalism's original ideals. Napoleon changes the commandments to suit his needs.

2) Napoleon becomes so similar to the humans that the animals can't tell them apart. Orwell's point was that Russia had suffered the same fate — Stalin's rule was no better than the Tsar's capitalist regime.

3) By making Animalism fail, Orwell was arguing that Russia had also failed in being fair and equal.

If only Napoleon had met Miss Piggy before Kermit had...

...he just needed the love of a good woman, that's all. Despite Napoleon's purges of the animals he claims have turned on Animalism, it's actually Napoleon who's most guilty, even breaking one of the key rules by killing other animals.

Education and Social Class

After the revolution, different <u>social classes</u> start to emerge. The pigs become the <u>ruling class</u>, and the other animals become the <u>working class</u> — a lack of education means they have <u>no power</u> and <u>do what they're told</u>.

Education Divides *the animals into* Social Classes

1) Two social classes form after the revolution, which <u>goes against</u> the commandment that "All animals are <u>equal</u>". The division is based on the animals' <u>intelligence</u>.

2) The pigs are the ruling class — they make <u>all the rules</u> because they can <u>write</u> them. The other animals accept that the pigs are "<u>cleverer</u>" and let them <u>take control</u>.

3) The pigs <u>reinforce</u> their status by taking up the symbols of <u>Man</u> — Napoleon appears "wearing an old bowler hat" and "with a pipe in his mouth".

Snowball and Napoleon Disagree *on* Education

1) The animals are supposed to be <u>equal</u>, but because the pigs <u>teach themselves to read</u>, they're <u>superior</u> from the start. By <u>controlling education</u>, they also control <u>who's</u> upper class.

2) Snowball and Napoleon have <u>different approaches </u>to education:

- Snowball wants to educate <u>all the animals</u> — he tries to teach them to read, write and <u>spread the ideas</u> of Animalism to everyone, so that there will be <u>true equality</u> among the animals.

- Napoleon is only interested in educating the <u>young</u>. He focuses on the <u>piglets</u> to continue the pigs' <u>superiority</u>, and the <u>puppies</u>, so that he can train them to be <u>loyal bodyguards</u>.

3) <u>Under Napoleon</u> the class system is likely to <u>stay the same</u> — he doesn't want to educate the other animals in case they use it to <u>rise up against him</u>. By only educating the pigs, they keep <u>all the power</u>.

The Animals Misuse *their* Education

1) The <u>uneducated</u> animals <u>remain working class</u> because they don't <u>make the most</u> of the education that Snowball offers them:

- Mollie only wants to learn how to <u>write her name</u>.

- Benjamin learns to read, but <u>refuses to use his ability</u>.

- Boxer wants to read and write, but can only <u>learn four letters</u>, which he is "<u>content with</u>".

© HALLMARK/TNT/ANIMAL FARM PRODUCTION
COURTESY THE KOBAL COLLECTION

2) Because of this <u>lack of interest</u> in education they remain <u>ignorant</u> and they can't work out anything for themselves.

3) The animals <u>accept everything</u> they're told and <u>submit</u> to the pigs' authority — they don't have the <u>intellect</u> to <u>object</u>.

I don't like to be a pig — but they do seem to get a better deal...

Knowledge is power in *Animal Farm*, but it only seems to get misused — the pigs use it to keep control, manipulate the others, and to brew alcohol. The other animals don't seem to care. Use your powers of learning for good...

Power and Language

Because the pigs are <u>educated</u>, they can <u>use language</u> to make the other animals <u>do what they want</u>. This is one of their main sources of <u>power</u>. You don't need brawn when you've got brains. I've got neither... *sigh*

Desire for **Power** Corrupts **Napoleon**

1) The whole point of Animalism (and communism) is <u>equality</u> — no one should have any more <u>power</u> than anyone else. When Napoleon seizes power on the farm, it shows how <u>corrupt</u> he is. The <u>more power</u> he has, the <u>more corrupt</u> he becomes and the more <u>Animalism is undermined</u>.

2) Napoleon <u>increases his power</u> over the farm by <u>controlling</u>:

Actions	**Thoughts**	**Theme — Language**
• By controlling <u>rations</u> • By using the <u>dogs</u> • Through trials and <u>executions</u>	• Through <u>language</u> • Using <u>propaganda</u> • Removing <u>democracy</u>	For <u>Orwell</u>, this was the <u>most dangerous</u> kind of control because it's so <u>difficult</u> to detect and <u>challenge</u>, especially by the <u>uneducated</u>.

Language is a **Powerful Tool**

1) Orwell was concerned about the <u>power of language</u>, and how it could be <u>manipulated</u> to change its <u>purpose</u> and <u>meaning</u>.

2) Squealer's <u>persuasive language</u> is a powerful form of <u>propaganda</u> (see p. 40). It reinforces Napoleon's <u>power</u>: "He was always referred to... as 'our leader, Comrade Napoleon'".

3) Boxer has <u>no power</u> because he can't <u>express</u> his feelings properly — when Snowball is exiled he can't "<u>think of anything to say</u>".

4) By <u>simplifying the commandments</u> to "Four legs good, two legs bad", Snowball causes the words to <u>lose their meaning</u>.

ПОД ВОДИТЕЛЬСТВОМ ВЕЛИКОГО СТАЛИНА–ВПЕРЕД К КОММУНИЗМУ!

An example of Stalin's propaganda: 'Under the Leadership of the Great Stalin — Forward to Communism!'

© Buyenlarge/Archive Photos /Getty Images

A totalitarian state is where the leaders have absolute power and control over the country.

There's no **Freedom** of **Speech**

1) Freedom of speech is necessary in an <u>equal</u>, <u>democratic society</u> — everyone has the right to a <u>fair say</u>.

2) However, when Snowball disagrees with Napoleon, he's <u>attacked</u> by the dogs and <u>banished</u> — there's no freedom of speech on Animal Farm.

Allegory

Trying to control peoples' <u>thoughts</u> is a feature of many <u>totalitarian</u> states.

3) Napoleon knows that <u>language is power</u>. By <u>ending</u> the Sunday meetings and <u>freedom of speech</u>, Napoleon <u>takes away</u> the other animals' power.

4) Even if an animal has a <u>rebellious thought</u>, they can't <u>express it</u>. Napoleon <u>controls their thoughts</u> by restricting what they <u>hear</u> and <u>say</u>.

Four legs good — writing essays bad...

... bad but necessary I'm afraid. By getting rid of free speech, Napoleon puts a stop to any resistance. If everyone's too scared to even speak, they won't consider rebelling. The cunning little piggy can then swoop in and steal all the power.

Propaganda

The pigs use propaganda to <u>control</u> the other animals and maintain <u>power</u>.
It's a further abuse of <u>language</u> and it's very dangerous in Squealer's hands. Or trotters.

The pigs use **Propaganda** *to* **Justify** *their* **Actions**

1) Propaganda is when an individual or group <u>spreads information</u> to make themselves <u>look good</u>.
   Often the information is <u>exaggerated</u> or <u>made up</u>. Napoleon uses it to <u>gain power</u> and <u>keep control</u>.

2) Squealer uses propaganda in <u>speeches</u> — he speaks "so persuasively" that the animals accept his words.
   He takes them aside and <u>convinces them</u> that the pigs' actions are <u>good</u> — this makes them <u>believe him</u>.

3) The pigs keep the animals loyal by <u>spreading</u> stories about how <u>cruelly</u> animals are treated on <u>other farms</u>.
   This means they <u>forget</u> the farm's own problems and are less likely to <u>rebel</u> against their masters.

Squealer uses **Propaganda** *to* **Twist** *the* **Truth**

Dictators spread <u>propaganda</u> to make themselves look <u>better</u>. Squealer uses <u>propaganda</u> to:

Glorify Napoleon

1) When anything good happens, Napoleon <u>takes credit</u> for it. He claims that the <u>windmill</u> was
   his idea, and the hens are <u>brainwashed</u> into giving him <u>credit</u> for how many eggs they've laid.

2) A weekly parade is held so that Napoleon can show off his <u>power</u> and <u>support</u>.

Blame Snowball

1) Squealer tells the animals that Snowball is their <u>real enemy</u> — this is a <u>clever lie</u> as it
   <u>unites them</u> against Snowball and makes them think that the other pigs are on their side.

2) The pigs use Snowball as a <u>scapegoat</u> and blame him for everything —
   "Whenever anything went wrong it became usual to attribute it to Snowball".

3) Even the animals' <u>memories</u> of Snowball aren't enough to <u>stop them believing</u> Squealer's <u>lies</u>.

The other animals **Spread It Too**

Soviet propaganda that shows Stalin hugging a child.

1) The pigs' propaganda is so <u>effective</u>, the animals
   not only <u>believe it</u>, they also <u>spread it themselves</u>:

   - Boxer unwittingly <u>spreads propaganda</u> every
     time he says "<u>Napoleon is always right</u>".

   - The pigeons <u>spread messages</u> like
     "<u>Death to Humanity</u>" and "Death to Frederick".

   - The sheep drown out <u>opposition</u> to Napoleon
     by chanting "<u>Four legs good two legs bad</u>".

2) By spreading <u>propaganda</u> themselves, the animals <u>seal their
   own fate</u>. They have become part of Napoleon's regime.

> **Theme — Education**
>
> Boxer's <u>lack of
> education</u> means he
> doesn't realise he's
> been <u>brainwashed</u>.

Repeat after me — I am the best, I am the best...

Propaganda is just a fancy word for boasting about yourself and what you've done, or lying about other people
to make yourself sound better in comparison. It's incredibly powerful if you can pull it off effectively...

Practice Questions

I love themes, they're so happy and catchy. It's the best bit about a lot of old TV shows. Everyone remembers the Batman theme, the A-Team theme, the — oh wait. That's theme *tunes* isn't it... Themes are the fun things that examiners like. Well they're not quite as fun as theme tunes, but these questions are. Honest.

Quick Questions

Q1   Who originally inspired Animalism:
a) Old Major   b) Snowball   c) Napoleon   d) Squealer?

Q2   How many rules of Animalism are there?

Q3   Which flag is the Animalism flag based on?

Q4   Which two pigs are the strongest leaders after the rebellion?

Q5   Why don't the other animals argue with the pigs?

Q6   List two ways that Squealer makes the other animals agree with him.

Q7   Give an example of what happens to one of the animals who speaks out against Napoleon?

Q8   What is propaganda?

Q9   Why do the pigs spread stories about how animals are treated on other farms?

In-depth Questions

Q1   Explain why you think Napoleon decides to stop freedom of speech on *Animal Farm*.

Q2   How does the pigs' education make them more powerful than the other animals?

Q3   Do you think the animals realise that the pigs are mistreating them, or are they unaware of it? Explain your answer, with examples from the text.

Q4   Why is it important that most of the working animals can't read and write?

Q5   Why do you think Snowball and Napoleon have different views on education?

Q6   How does Napoleon control the animals' thoughts in the novel?

Q7   In what ways do the working animals spread Napoleon's propaganda themselves?

Practice Questions

The further into the section you get, the more serious I get. The last page was *quite* serious, so I'm really going to have to go overboard on this one to make it even more serious. Here are some exam questions that you should answer in preparation for your examination. Try to answer them as if you really were in the exam so that means full answers. No peeking. Eyes down, pens up and silence please... (I think that was serious enough).

Exam-Style Questions

1   How does Orwell present Napoleon's changing attitudes to Animalism in two different chapters?

2   Read the passage that begins "Napoleon stood up" (midway through Chapter Five) and ends with "crept back into the barn". With reference to this passage explore the importance of power in *Animal Farm*.

3   Think about two events in the novel that reflect the problems of a social class system. Write about:
   •   what happens in the events.
   •   how Orwell presents social class in these events through the way he writes.

4   How does Orwell present the importance of education in *Animal Farm*?

5   How does Orwell vividly portray the dangers of propaganda in *Animal Farm*?

The Structure of 'Animal Farm'

The animals start off being <u>oppressed</u> by a drunk, neglectful master — they end up being <u>oppressed</u> by a drunk, neglectful master. You've got to wonder if it was all <u>worth while</u>...

Animal Farm has a Chronological Structure

1) *Animal Farm* has a simple <u>structure</u>, like most <u>fairy stories</u> (see p. 45). The events are described in <u>chronological</u> order (the order they happen) so the story is <u>easy to follow</u>.

2) The chronological structure lets the reader see the <u>gradual decline</u> of Animalism. It shows Napoleon taking control by <u>slowly undermining</u> each commandment in turn.

The Events of the novel are Cyclical

1) The story is <u>cyclical</u> — the end the novel is very <u>similar</u> to the beginning. Orwell <u>hints</u> at this ending throughout the book, so there's a sense of <u>inevitability</u> about the revolution's <u>failure</u>.

2) Orwell uses the farm's <u>name</u> to show the revolution's <u>progress</u>. Under Jones, the farm is called 'Manor Farm'. When the animals are free from Jones it becomes 'Animal Farm'. When Napoleon renames it 'The Manor Farm', it shows that the revolution has <u>failed</u>.

3) The final chapter shows the pigs "<u>melting</u>" and changing into men. The animals can barely <u>distinguish</u> between the <u>two</u>.

© HALLMARK/TNT/ANIMAL FARM PRODUCTION
COURTESY THE KOBAL COLLECTION

> The message is loud and clear — <u>watch your leaders</u> because too much power can <u>corrupt</u> people (and pigs).

History starts to Repeat Itself

There's lots of <u>repetition</u> — it <u>links</u> the events together and shows that the new regime is <u>mirroring</u> the old:

Jones is a <u>drunk</u> — "drinking more than was good for him". The book <u>starts</u> with him returning from the pub, drunk.		Napoleon becomes a <u>drunk</u>. The book <u>ends</u> with him drinking, telling his guests to fill their "glasses to the brim".
Old Major teaches the animals 'Beasts of England'. It's a <u>revolutionary</u> song that's meant to <u>inspire</u> the animals.		After 'Beasts of England' is banned, it's still "hummed secretly" by the animals as a <u>private</u> act of <u>rebellion</u> and hope.
Old Major warns Boxer that when he is old, Mr Jones will <u>sell</u> him to the knacker's yard where he will be killed.		When Boxer becomes ill, Napoleon <u>sells</u> him to the knacker's yard and buys whisky for the pigs with the money.

Cyclical events — makes me feel a bit queasy...

Orwell uses a cyclical structure in his novel to show how history repeated itself in Russia — the peasants and workers suffered under the Tsar, overthrew him, only to suffer under Stalin too. There aren't many happy endings in history.

Allegory and Fable

Animal Farm isn't just a story about some mean pigs — Orwell is trying to <u>teach</u> the reader about <u>corrupt</u> communism using a variety of <u>literary techniques</u>.

Animal Farm is an *Allegory*

1) An <u>allegory</u> is a story that uses its <u>characters</u> and <u>events</u> as symbols for <u>something else</u>.

2) It's <u>easier</u> for readers of all ages to <u>understand</u> an allegory, rather than a complicated political novel.

3) *Animal Farm* is an allegory for <u>corrupt communism</u>, particularly the Soviet Union under Stalin. However the story's location is general — it could've happened <u>anywhere</u> so it has universal <u>appeal</u>.

4) The <u>repetitive events</u> of the novel <u>symbolise</u> the way that one regime was <u>replaced</u> by another in Russia.

Jones and *Napoleon Symbolise All Dictators*

A dictator is someone who has complete control of a country.

The <u>parallels</u> between Napoleon and Jones show how far Napoleon has <u>betrayed</u> Animalism.

- Mr Jones and Napoleon are both <u>cruel</u> and <u>evil</u>. They <u>represent</u> all tyrannical <u>dictators</u> in history.

- Mr Jones has a <u>common name</u> and <u>no real character</u> — he could be <u>anyone</u>.

- Napoleon turns into Mr Jones despite old Major's warning that they "must not come to resemble" Man. This suggests that all dictators are essentially the <u>same</u> — greedy, selfish and cruel.

The *Animals* Symbolise *Inequality*

1) The working animals are symbolic of the <u>peasants</u> and <u>workers</u> of Soviet Russia who thought their lives would <u>improve</u> after the revolution.

2) In a more general way, they also symbolise any community who have <u>no power</u> against their leader.

3) They symbolise <u>inequality</u> in a totalitarian society.

Russian peasants go to work in the fields during collectivisation (see p.10).

The novel is a *Beast Fable*

1) *Animal Farm* is a <u>beast fable</u> — a short story that uses <u>animals</u> to teach a <u>moral lesson</u>.

By using <u>animals</u> as the main characters, Orwell increases the <u>effectiveness</u> of the novel. It makes the politicians that he's <u>satirising</u> look <u>ridiculous</u>.

2) By using animals instead of real people, the story appeals to a <u>wider audience</u>, whilst still passing on a <u>political</u> message.

3) The animals are <u>symbols</u> and most aren't fully <u>rounded</u> characters.

4) Most beast fables end with a clear moral but the animals learn <u>nothing</u> in *Animal Farm*. The novel comes <u>full-circle</u>, it's <u>uncertain</u> whether the animals realise this or not.

Babe 3 — Porkers in Power...

You will almost certainly have to write about how *Animal Farm* is one big, massive allegory for Russia. Even if they try and disguise it by asking you to write about 'society' or 'history' alarm bells should go off. When in doubt, allegory.

Narrative Style

Animal Farm isn't narrated by a <u>specific</u> character — this stops it from being a <u>personal</u> account. It's more like a business account with a platinum card of <u>evil</u> and high interest rates of <u>death</u>.

The **Narrator** doesn't **Directly Influence** the **Reader**

The narrator uses <u>simple</u>, <u>unemotional language</u>, and only describes what the working animals see. As a result, the reader's view of the farm is <u>restricted</u>, and you're left to make up your <u>own mind</u> about what's happening. The narrator is:

- <u>Detached</u> — the anonymous narrator's thoughts are <u>controlled</u> and <u>detached</u> so that the reader isn't directly influenced. This is <u>important</u> since one of the book's themes is the <u>twisting of language</u>.

- <u>Limited</u> — the narrator usually says <u>no more</u> than what the animals <u>see</u> and <u>hear</u>. The reader <u>relies</u> on the narrator for information — just as the animals rely on the pigs.

The Narrator just **Gives** the **Reader** the **Facts**

1) The story is told from the <u>working animals'</u> point of view — occasionally Orwell shifts the narration to an animal's perspective e.g. Clover. This suggests that Orwell's <u>sympathies</u> lie with the <u>working classes</u>.

2) Telling the story more from the working animal's perspective shows how <u>naive</u> they are. The reader <u>understands</u> things that the animals don't.

3) Whereas the reader draws <u>conclusions</u> from what the narrator does (or doesn't) say, the animals <u>fail</u> to learn anything from the events of the novel.

Although Orwell criticises the way that the pigs manipulate language, his own language choices can manipulate the reader.

Orwell Describes things **Matter-of-Factly**

1) Orwell describes things <u>briefly</u>. This <u>simple</u> writing style makes the narrator seem more <u>trustworthy</u>.

2) The narrative is <u>detached</u> rather than emotional, e.g. the slaughtered animals are described simply as a "pile of corpses".

3) The lack of <u>reaction</u> from the narrator makes the terrifying events being described seem even more <u>shocking</u>.

4) The simplistic language <u>contrasts</u> with the horrific events, e.g. the betrayal of Boxer.

5) It also gives the novel a <u>broader appeal</u> — the language is more <u>entertaining</u> and less <u>challenging</u> than a historical explanation.

HORSE SLAUGHTERER

The full title of the book is *Animal Farm: A Fairy Story*. The <u>simple</u> language <u>suits</u> the fairy tale genre but it <u>contrasts</u> greatly with the brutal treatment and suffering of the animals.

What do you get when you cross a pig with tyranny...

Napoleon, obviously. Or a tyranig. No matter what question you get in the exam you can always add a bit about narrative style to impress the examiner, so make sure you revise this page well and learn all the technical terms.

Satire and Irony

How would you describe the taste of iron filings? <u>Irony</u>. What instrument do mechanics play? A <u>satire</u>. What do you call jokes about literary techniques? <u>Rubbish</u>.

Irony can make a **Serious Point**

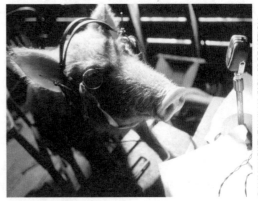

© HALLMARK/TNT/ANIMAL FARM PRODUCTION
COURTESY THE KOBAL COLLECTION

1) <u>Irony</u> is when you say one thing but mean the <u>opposite</u>.

2) The subtitle of the book, "A Fairy Story", is ironic. In fairy stories the 'good' characters usually live happily ever after, but there's <u>no happy ending</u> for the animals — there's a sense of <u>inevitability</u> that the revolution will fail.

3) Squealer's language is often <u>ironic</u>, e.g. "you do not imagine, I hope, that we pigs are doing this in the spirit of selfishness". Orwell uses irony to show how words can <u>lose their meaning</u>.

Orwell uses **Dramatic Irony**

Dramatic irony is when the reader realises the significance of what a character says or does before any of the characters in the novel.

<u>Dramatic irony</u> emphasises the animals' <u>ignorance</u> of how much Napoleon takes advantage of them.

- The pigs start to <u>resemble</u> the humans they rebelled against. The reader sees this from the <u>beginning</u> when the pigs steal the milk and apples.

- The pigs pretend that they haven't broken any of the (changed) commandments — but the reader <u>remembers</u> exactly what the original commandments were.

Satire makes things seem **Ridiculous**

1) <u>Satire</u> makes fun of <u>people</u> or <u>ideas</u>. It does this by exaggerating them or making them seem ridiculous. Satire is often <u>funny</u>, but makes a <u>serious point</u>.

2) It often has a <u>political motivation</u>. *Animal Farm* is a <u>satirical attack</u> on the Soviet Union. Comparing political figures to pigs is satirical because it makes them seem <u>absurd</u>.

3) In *Animal Farm* it's not just the leaders being <u>satirised</u> — the workers also seem <u>foolish</u>. For example the Russian people who failed to speak out against the corruption are satirised as <u>sheep</u>.

Context
The book's <u>satirical attack</u> on the Soviet Union meant Orwell struggled to find a publisher who would <u>risk</u> publishing something so <u>controversial</u>.

4) Satire makes some events in *Animal Farm* <u>darkly humorous</u> because they seem so ridiculous, e.g. when the pigs dress in human clothes. It allows Orwell to <u>disguise</u> his criticisms rather than condemning communism <u>directly</u> — it sounds less <u>preachy</u> and more <u>appealing</u>.

Dramatic irony —isn't that when you use a clothes press on stage...

Animal Farm isn't a laugh-a-minute, rib-tickling tale because that would've diluted Orwell's themes and messages. It does have moments of dark humour though, which are used to make the satire even stronger. Hilarious, I know.

How the Characters Speak

The language the animals use is symbolic of their place in the social hierarchy. The better educated the animal, the more sophisticated their language use. My hamster went to Oxford and talks like the Queen.

Simple Characters *use* Repetitive Language

© iStockphoto.com/Christopher Mansfield

1) The sheep are manipulated by the pigs and have no ideas of their own. They simply repeat "Four legs good, two legs bad" to drown out debate.

2) Boxer repeats "I will work harder", showing he is unable to think for himself.

3) The repetitive language shows how easily the uneducated characters are brainwashed by slogans and propaganda.

> Repetitive language is often used in fairy stories. Orwell uses it here to show how far the animals have been manipulated.

Powerful Characters *use* Persuasive Language

1) Old Major uses political and rhetorical language. He uses emotional appeals, e.g. "I feel it my duty", lists of three and rhetorical questions. The animals listen to him "attentively".

2) Snowball uses emotional language — he makes a "passionate appeal" about the windmill. He's a skilled speaker, which makes him a threat to Napoleon.

3) Squealer is the master of persuasive language. He's able to make the other animals believe anything by distorting facts, rewriting history and twisting words (see p. 28).

As Napoleon Gains *more* Authority, *so does his* Language

1) At first Napoleon is "not much of a talker". As the novel progresses, he makes increasingly political speeches using persuasive techniques that the animals can't argue with.

2) His language also becomes more creative as he blames Snowball, e.g. saying that the destruction of the windmill was revenge for his "expulsion" by Napoleon.

3) Napoleon and Squealer patronise the others. They call the other animals "comrades", which makes the animals feel equal but the reader recognises the irony — they are never treated as equals.

> **Theme — Language**
>
> Orwell uses the characters to show how powerful and influential language can be.

4) Napoleon's made up titles reinforce his leadership, e.g. "father of all animals". These are ironic because they're based on lies.

Napoleon was Russian here, there and everywhere...

Well, he wasn't really — he was pigging out on whisky and apples, but the joke wouldn't have worked otherwise. What do you mean 'what joke?' Make sure you learn the significance of the characters and how they speak.

The Setting of 'Animal Farm'

Life on the farm isn't all straw chewin', barn dances and hoedowns. It's actually an <u>allegory</u> for Russia, only with less vodka, dancing bears and men in fuzzy hats and more whisky-drinking pigs.

The Setting **Symbolises** the **Soviet Union...**

Theme — Social Class

The ruling class (the pigs) use <u>intelligence</u> to create a <u>social divide</u> between themselves and the working classes (the other animals).

1) The events of the book reflect what happened in <u>Russia</u> in the early twentieth century (see Section One).

2) The farmhouse is where the <u>ruling class</u> live — it's full of "<u>unbelievable luxury</u>" to represent the palaces of wealthy Russians. When the pigs move into the farmhouse, it shows that old Major's <u>warning</u> about becoming human has been <u>ignored</u>.

Context

Orwell never condemns the pigs' actions <u>outright</u>, he's careful to <u>protect</u> himself as an author — he didn't want to risk a <u>Russian backlash</u>.

3) The working animals live in much <u>worse conditions</u> — there's <u>less food</u> and <u>little comfort</u>. This represents the quality of life for many Russians under Stalin.

...but it could **Apply** to **Any Country**

1) The setting of the farm is <u>symbolic</u> and the location is <u>general</u> — it could be <u>anywhere</u>. Orwell suggests that the novel's events could, and did, happen <u>all over the world</u>.

2) The realistic descriptions of everyday farm life <u>contrast</u> with Napoleon's terrifying behaviour. It shows that dictators can affect <u>ordinary workers</u>.

3) The chapters near the beginning are set in the summer — this represents the initial <u>optimism</u> of the rebellion. Towards the end, several chapters are set in the "bitter winter". This reflects the animals' <u>suffering</u> and the increasingly <u>bad</u> outlook for the rebellion.

The **Windmill** is part of the **Animals' Struggle**

1) At first, the windmill is part of a <u>wonderful vision</u> of the <u>future</u>. It will "light the stalls and warm them in winter".

2) Snowball and Napoleon <u>disagree</u> about building the windmill. Napoleon's lies about the windmill <u>damage</u> what it stood for.

3) The windmill is "slow" and "laborious" to build. It is also <u>pointless</u> — it's repeatedly <u>destroyed</u> and <u>rebuilt</u>. It symbolises the increasing <u>failure</u> of old Major's dream, and the <u>impossibility</u> of Animalism.

4) When the windmill is rebuilt after the Battle of the Windmill, it's used to mill corn because it's more <u>profitable</u> than generating electricity — the pigs care more about <u>capitalism</u> than <u>equality</u>.

© iStockphoto.com/RelaxFoto.de

Animal Farm — it was almost all(e) gory...

Orwell was deliberately vague and general about the setting so that his message could be applied to any totalitarian state, although it was pretty obvious that he'd taken his inspiration from events in Russia.

Symbolism in 'Animal Farm'

Songs and chants are used at the start of the book to <u>unite</u> the animals and spread the message of Animalism. By the end of the book, they're used to <u>control</u> and <u>brainwash</u>.

*'Beasts of England' is the **Anthem** for the **Revolution***

1) Old Major's ideals are <u>summarised</u> and <u>passed on</u> through the "stirring" song 'Beasts of England'.

2) At the start, it represents the revolution — it's <u>patriotic</u> and <u>inspiring</u>. It reflects the hope that the animals will be <u>free</u>.

3) As Napoleon becomes more tyrannical, singing the song <u>unites</u> the animals and gives them <u>hope</u>.

4) Towards the end, Napoleon <u>bans</u> 'Beasts of England', claiming it no longer had "any purpose" since the rebellion had finished — this shows that he has completely <u>discarded</u> the ideals of Animalism.

*Napoleon uses **Songs** as **Propaganda***

Theme — Education

The <u>less-educated</u> characters such as Boxer and the sheep are the ones who are most <u>influenced</u> by the slogans and the propaganda.

1) Napoleon has <u>poems</u> written to remind the animals that he's in <u>charge</u> and to make himself sound good. In one poem he's described as "giver of / All that thy creatures love".

2) Using songs and chants is an effective way of <u>reinforcing</u> his power, especially to the <u>less-educated</u> animals who may not <u>understand</u> speeches or be able to read.

3) Spreading propaganda through song is <u>subtle</u> — the songs are taken up by the animals, who sing without <u>thinking</u> about the meaning.

*The **Rituals** become **Meaningless***

At the start, the animals introduce rituals to celebrate their <u>achievements</u>. By the end, these are <u>worthless</u>.

At the start of the book, <u>medals</u> are given to animals who have been hurt or killed in battle. They show recognition for <u>bravery</u>.

Later, Napoleon simply awards himself the 'Order of the Green Banner' for nothing — it has become <u>worthless</u>.

Rituals such as firing the gun on the anniversary of the rebellion are established to create a sense of <u>honour</u> and <u>pride</u>.

The animals take part in weekly "Spontaneous Demonstrations" where poems are read in honour of Napoleon. Rituals have become a way for Napoleon to <u>celebrate himself</u>.

Titles and rituals are used to <u>unite</u> the animals and <u>reward</u> them for their <u>commitment</u> to Animalism.

Titles and rituals become <u>worthless</u>, a way for Napoleon to <u>elevate</u> himself above the other animals and maintain <u>control</u>.

Have a proper gander at this page...

If you get a question on symbolism it's always worthwhile mentioning a less-obvious example like the songs and rituals to make your answer really stand out and impress the examiner rather than the same old examplezzzzzzzzzzzzzzzz.

Symbolism in 'Animal Farm'

Orwell wrote *Animal Farm* in a <u>plain</u> style, but that doesn't mean he didn't use clever <u>literary techniques</u> like <u>symbolism</u>. Here's a few to start you off, but there are <u>plenty</u> of other examples that you can discuss in the <u>exam</u>.

Symbols of *Slavery* are used by pigs and humans

1) The song 'Beasts of England' lists the symbols of <u>slavery</u> — rings, harnesses, bits, spurs and whips.

Symbolism is when an object is used to represent a theme or idea without mentioning it directly.

2) After the revolution, these symbols of oppression are "flung down the well". This symbolises the animals <u>breaking free</u> from slavery. It makes them feel free even though they are still <u>following orders</u>.

3) By the end of the novel Napoleon is carrying a <u>whip</u>. This symbolises that things have <u>returned</u> to how they used to be.

The *Guns* symbolise *Violence*

1) At the start of the book, humans use <u>guns</u> to <u>control</u> the animals. After the revolution the animals <u>destroy</u> them because the guns were part of the animals' <u>oppression</u>.

2) After the Battle of the Cowshed, the gun Mr Jones leaves becomes <u>symbolic</u> — it's set up by the flagpole to represent the animal's <u>victory</u> over the old regime. It's fired twice a year to mark the anniversary of the battle and the rebellion.

3) When Napoleon takes up <u>weapons</u> again it's a sign that he has become more <u>humanised</u>. He also wants to use guns to <u>control</u> the animals.

4) The animals initially use <u>violence</u> to achieve <u>change</u>, but even after they <u>succeed</u> in overthrowing Jones it remains in their <u>society</u>. Orwell uses Napoleon's violent behaviour to show that this is <u>dangerous</u>.

The *Flag* symbolises the animals' *Freedom*

The crossed horn and hoof on the Animalism flag.

1) The flag is a symbol of the animals' <u>freedom</u>.

2) The green symbolises "the green fields", and the <u>hoof</u> and <u>horn</u> represent the <u>unity</u> of the animals.

3) In the final chapter the hoof and horn are <u>removed</u> from the flag — "It would be a plain green flag from now onwards". This symbolises that the working animals no longer have any <u>power</u>.

Allegory

The <u>hammer</u> and <u>sickle</u> on the flag of the Soviet Union (see p. 37 for this flag) represents the <u>workers</u> and <u>peasants</u>. It became a <u>meaningless</u> symbol of workers' power.

Your yawn symbolises that you're bored by revision...

Hurrah! Another section almost finished. There's just a few questions on the next page to make sure you know it all and then it's only Section 6 standing between you and freedom. Well, other than the exam, of course.

Practice Questions

These questions shouldn't prove too tricky, unless you want them to be tricky. In which case may I suggest translating them into Swahili and answering them through the medium of interpretative dance.

Quick Questions

Q1 What does 'chronological structure' mean?

Q2 List three things at the end of the book that echo how they were at the beginning.

Q3 Summarise the message of the book in less than five words.

Q4 A story that is written to represent something else is called: a) an allegory, or b) an allegedly?

Q5 Give two examples of how *Animal Farm* is similar to a fairy story.

Q6 Whose perspective is the story told from?

Q7 What is irony?

Q8 What do the whips symbolise?

In-depth Questions

Q1 How does Napoleon's language change over the course of *Animal Farm*?

Q2 How do you think Orwell uses language to make you sympathise with the working animals? Include at least three examples in your answer.

Q3 Give three examples of repetitive language in the novel.

Q4 Give two examples of irony in *Animal Farm* and explain how they are effective.

Q5 What reasons might Orwell have for setting the novel in a commonplace farm?

Section Five — The Writer's Techniques

Practice Questions

You should know the drill by now. Pick a question, set a timer then plan, scribble, check. Make sure you write full answers and include quotes and analysis to prepare you properly for the exam.
On your marks, get set, GO...

Exam-Style Questions

1   How does Orwell present the changed attitudes and behaviour of the pigs in Chapter 10 in comparison to Chapter 2?

2   How does Orwell use allegory to explore the meaning of real historical events in *Animal Farm*?

3   What techniques does Orwell use to make his satire effective?

4   Read the last two paragraphs of Chapter 3 from "'Comrades!' he cried. 'You do not imagine'". How does Orwell present the relationship between Squealer and the other animals in this extract?

5   How does Orwell use *Animal Farm*'s narrative style to explore the importance of language?

6   How important do you think the windmill is in highlighting the problems of Animalism?

7   How does Orwell use symbolism in *Animal Farm* to explore ideas about power?

Assessment Advice

This section will help you write a <u>scorching essay</u>, more scorching than, say, Brad Pitt walking across a bed of hot coals to cook a curry.

The exam questions will test **Four Main Skills**

The examiner will be looking for you to show that you can:

1) Write about the text in a <u>thoughtful way</u> — <u>pick out</u> appropriate <u>examples</u> and <u>quotations</u> to back up your opinions.

2) <u>Identify and explain</u> features of the book's <u>form</u>, <u>structure</u> and <u>language</u>. Show how Orwell uses these to present the <u>ideas</u>, <u>themes</u>, <u>characters</u> and <u>settings</u> effectively.

3) <u>Link</u> the story to its <u>cultural, social and historical background</u> (i.e. the Soviet Union under Stalin). You need to understand the <u>impact</u> and <u>influence</u> the book has had.

4) Write in a <u>clear</u>, <u>well-structured</u> way. Good <u>spelling, grammar, punctuation</u> and <u>paragraphing</u> will help you get the top marks.

Read the Question **Carefully** and **Underline Key Words**

1) The style of question you'll get depends on which <u>exam board</u> you're sitting. If you're studying the book for <u>Controlled Assessment</u>, this section's still worth a look — it'll help you with your <u>essay structure</u>.

| AQA | You'll get a <u>choice of two essay questions</u> (without extracts) and you'll have to <u>pick one</u> (unless you're doing foundation, in which case you'll have to do <u>both</u>). |

| OCR | There will be <u>two questions</u> for you to choose from. One will ask you to comment on an <u>extract</u> from the book which will be <u>provided</u> in the exam. The other question will be an <u>essay question</u> about the novel as a <u>whole</u>. |

| Edexcel | You'll be asked <u>questions</u> about a passage <u>provided</u> in the exam as well as the <u>wider novel</u>. |

2) <u>Read</u> the question at least <u>twice</u> so you completely understand it. <u>Underline</u> the key words.

Here's an exam-style question

Think about the <u>way</u> he speaks, his actions and how he's <u>described</u>.

Make sure you concentrate on <u>Napoleon</u> — don't write too much about any of the other characters.

This is a big hint — you've got to explain how Napoleon's character <u>develops</u>.

Q1   <u>How</u> does the character of <u>Napoleon</u> <u>change</u> over the <u>course of *Animal Farm*</u>?

You should consider the <u>society</u> represented in the novel in your answer.

This question is telling you to write about the <u>social background</u> of the novel — you've <u>got to do that</u> to get top marks.

You've got to include points from the very <u>beginning</u> right through to the <u>end</u>.

The advice squad — the best cops in the NYPD...

Whichever specification you're doing, the question is likely to touch on the main themes, characters and social, cultural and historical background of the book. All the stuff you've been revising in fact. Pretty handy, that.

Structure and Planning

It's easy to panic under pressure — all the more reason to spend 5 minutes jotting down a <u>cunning plan</u> for what you're going to write. It'll give you time to think and give your answer a better <u>structure</u>.

Plan your answer before you start

1) If you plan, you're less likely to forget something <u>important</u>.

2) Write your plan at the <u>top of your answer booklet</u> and draw a <u>neat line</u> through it when you've finished.

3) <u>Don't</u> spend <u>too long</u> on your plan. It's only <u>rough work</u>, so you don't need to write in full sentences. Here are a few <u>examples</u> of different ways you can plan your answer:

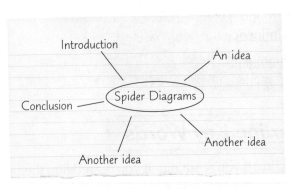

Bullet points and headings...
- Intro...
- An idea...
- The next idea...

Tables with...

A point...	Quote to back this up...
Another point...	Quote...
A different point...	Quote...
A brand new point...	Quote...

4) A good plan will help you <u>organise</u> your ideas — and write a good, <u>well-structured</u> essay.

Structure your answer

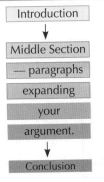

Introduction → Middle Section — paragraphs expanding your argument. → Conclusion

1) Your <u>introduction</u> should give a brief answer to the question you're writing about. Make it clear how you're going to <u>tackle the topic</u>.

2) The <u>middle section</u> of your essay should explain your answer in detail and give evidence to back it up. Write a <u>paragraph</u> for each point you make. Start the paragraph by making the <u>point</u>, then <u>back it up</u> with <u>evidence</u> — examples and quotations from *Animal Farm*.

3) Remember to write a <u>conclusion</u> — a paragraph at the end which <u>sums up</u> your <u>main points</u>.

Structure your answer or Napoleon will get you.

Don't Panic if you make a Mistake

1) Okay, so say the exam is going well and you've timed it beautifully. Instead of putting your feet up on the desk for the last 5 minutes, it's a good idea to <u>read through</u> your <u>answers</u> at the end and <u>correct any mistakes</u>...

2) If you want to get rid of something, just <u>cross it out</u>. <u>Don't scribble</u> over it.

3) If you've <u>left stuff out</u> write it in a separate section at the end of the essay. Put a <u>star</u> (*) next to both the extra <u>writing</u> and the <u>place</u> you want it to go.

To plan or not to plan, that is the question...
The answer is yes, yes, a thousand times yes. Often students dive right in, worried that planning will take up valuable time. But 5 minutes spent organising a well-structured answer is loads better than pages of waffle. Mmm waffles.

Sample Exam Question

And now the bit you've all been waiting for — a sample exam question and a lovely little plan.
Go make yourself a cup of tea, settle down and enjoy.

Here's a **Sample Exam Question**

Read this feisty exam question. That's the best way to start...

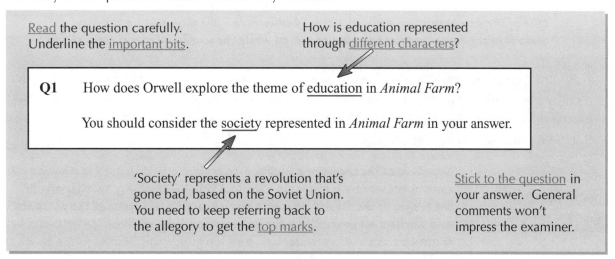

Read the question carefully.
Underline the important bits.

How is education represented
through different characters?

Q1   How does Orwell explore the theme of education in *Animal Farm*?

You should consider the society represented in *Animal Farm* in your answer.

'Society' represents a revolution that's
gone bad, based on the Soviet Union.
You need to keep referring back to
the allegory to get the top marks.

Stick to the question in
your answer. General
comments won't
impress the examiner.

Here's how you could **Plan** your **Answer**...

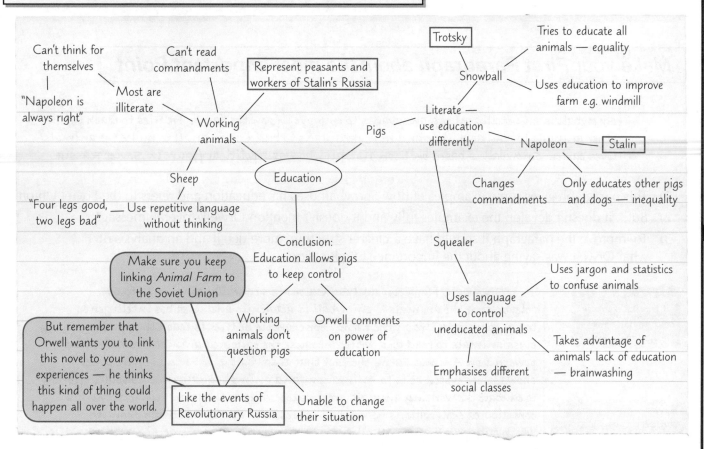

What do examiners eat? Why, egg-sam-wiches of course...

The most important thing to remember is DON'T PANIC. Take a deep breath, read the questions, pick a good 'un,
write a plan... take another deep breath... and you're ready to start writing. Leave 5 minutes at the end to check too.

Worked Answer

These pages will show you how to take an okay answer and turn it into a really good one.

Use your **Introduction** to get off to a **Good Start**

These pages are all about how to word your sentences to impress the examiner, so we haven't included everything from the plan on page 55.

You might start with something like...

> One of the key themes of Animal Farm is education. The pigs end up taking control of the farm because they are educated while the uneducated animals suffer.

1) This intro is okay. It mentions the division in power between the educated and uneducated animals.

2) It's also a good idea to use the key words in the question to give your essay focus and show the examiner you're on track and that you're thinking about the question from the start.

3) But there's still room for improvement...

This intro talks about the author's message and the historical context.

> Orwell uses the theme of education to explore how it is used to divide and control the working animals. He does this by creating an allegory of the events of the Soviet Union to show how Stalin oppressed the peasants and workers by controlling the information they received. Orwell uses key characters to show how education and language can be used to overpower an uneducated working class.

This tells the examiner what the essay's about and shows that you've thought about your essay structure.

Make your **First Paragraph** about the most **Important Point**

> Snowball is an intelligent pig and wants to improve life on the farm. He tries to teach the other animals to read and write and he makes plans to build a windmill to make the animals' lives easier. Snowball is based on Leon Trotsky who was a political figure in Soviet Russia.

1) This paragraph gives some examples of how Snowball uses his education and refers to the Soviet Union.

2) But... it doesn't develop the examples fully and it doesn't mention Orwell's overall message.

3) To improve the paragraph it should have a clearer structure, more detail and an analysis of what Orwell was saying about the importance of education.

This is a good start — it tells the examiner which characters you're going to talk about.

This bit makes a good point about education and power.

> Snowball, Napoleon and Squealer are generally considered to be "cleverest of the animals". Snowball is academic and uses his intelligence to try to improve life on the farm. For example he tries to teach the working class animals to read and write. Because the educated animals were the most powerful on Animal Farm, the fact that Snowball is willing to share power shows how devoted he is to Animalism and animal equality. Snowball's efforts to educate the working animals are unsuccessful as they don't understand his complicated explanations. Snowball is presented as a sympathetic character which suggests that Orwell believed in the importance of literacy in a fair society.

Make sure you keep referring to Orwell — he was trying to make some important points about the power of education and language.

Worked Answer

You need to make a Variety of Points

After you've talked about the pigs you might start your next point like this:

> The working animals represent the workers and peasants of Soviet Russia.
> They are uneducated and are easily manipulated by the clever pigs.

1) It introduces the working animals and shows the <u>similarities</u> between them and the Russian workers.

2) You can make this paragraph better by giving more <u>detailed examples</u> and backing up points with <u>quotes</u>.

> *Linking words show you're changing topics and makes the structure clearer.*

> However, the other animals are less educated and represent the working classes of the Soviet Union. They have no power and believe what they are told without questioning it, for example Boxer repeats "Napoleon is always right". His repetitive language shows that he can't think for himself and has been manipulated by the pigs so that he won't oppose them.

> *Make sure you use a range of quotes, but don't quote huge chunks. Keep them snappy and relevant.*

3) You could develop it by describing how Orwell uses some of the <u>minor characters</u> to explore education:

> Not all the working animals on the farm are uneducated. Benjamin can read and write but he refuses to "meddle in such matters" because he doesn't want to get involved or cause trouble. He seems to have accepted that Animalism will fail. When Benjamin does finally use his education to read the side of the knacker's van, it's too late because he can't do anything to help Boxer.

> *Including a bit about minor characters makes you stand out because it shows how well you know the novel.*

Finish your essay in Style

You could say:

> In conclusion, Animal Farm deals with the theme of education by showing that the educated pigs have control over the uneducated animals at the end of the novel. This shows the reader how important education is.

1) This conclusion is okay, but it doesn't summarise <u>how</u> Orwell <u>explores</u> the theme or social setting.

2) So to make it really <u>impressive</u> you could say something like...

> Animal Farm is an allegory of the events of Soviet Russia. It shows the reader how important education is in a democratic society. Napoleon only allows the pigs and the dogs to learn to read and write leaving the other animals uneducated and powerless. Only Snowball tries to educate the other animals but this soon stops when he is chased off the farm. Orwell shows how an educated elite can control others, but also how the uneducated workers allow themselves to be controlled because of their inability to think for themselves.

> *This summarises how Orwell uses the characters to explore the theme.*

> *Make your last sentence really stand out — it's your last opportunity to impress the examiner.*

Why do alligators write good essays? Because their quotes are snappy...

It seems like there's a lot to remember on these two pages, but there's not really. To summarise — write a good intro and conclusion, make a good range of points (one per paragraph) and put your most important point in paragraph one. Easy.

Index

The Characters in 'Animal Farm'

Phew! You should be an expert on *Animal Farm* by now. But if you want a bit of light relief and a quick recap of the novel's plot, sit yourself down and read through *Animal Farm — The Cartoon...*

George Orwell's 'Animal Farm'